FORGOTTEN FATHERS

$3.75

FORGOTTEN
FATHERS

By Edward Pinkowski

MEET THE AUTHOR

Edward Pinkowski was born in Holyoke, Massachusetts, and moved to Pennsylvania with his parents when he was fourteen. He was graduated from Mount Carmel High School and contributed to a number of periodicals before entering the Navy early in World War II. He spent most of his time in Washington, D. C., with a Navy writers' project. After the war he returned to free lance writing and subsequently started a small newspaper at Bridgeport, Pa. Eventually he left it to finish a book, WASHINGTON'S OFFICERS SLEPT HERE, dealing with the houses in which Washington and his officers were quartered at the time of the Valley Forge encampment.

MEET THE ARTIST

His full name is Theodore Edward Charles Kunda, but he prefers to sign his art work with his initials only. That came about in 1938 when he won an art prize upon graduation from Upper Merion High School. One of his teachers suggested the use of TEC. After attending the Philadelphia Museum School of Industrial Art, he became the first of three brothers to win wings in the Army Air Force. On his sixteenth bombing mission over Europe he was shot down and spent eleven months in a German prison camp. Less than a year after his liberation he went into the commercial sign painting business at Norristown.

FORGOTTEN FATHERS

BY EDWARD PINKOWSKI

Author of

WASHINGTON'S OFFICERS SLEPT HERE

Portraits by

TEC KUNDA

SUNSHINE PRESS

1731 Vine Street   . Philadelphia

Manufactured in the United States of America

TO
EDWARD H. SCHMIDT
Associate Editor, The Reader's Digest
in gratitude

19150

Preface

The men I have featured in this book started
something new in American life for which few
persons remember them today. Never, in fact,
did these fathers gain as much recognition as
they deserve. Their contributions in the field of
sports, science, religion, journalism, education,
architecture, medicine, entertainment, traffic
control, banking, commerce and industry had a
lot to do with making this country heterodoxical.
The *Dictionary of American Biography*, which
boasts that it "is an epitome of our national life
in all its varied aspects," lists only seven of these
fathers as subjects of biographies in the twenty
volumes of its double-columned pages. The
others are almost as forgotten as the pilot who
dropped the atomic bomb on Hiroshima.

How many people know, for example, that
Dr. Matthew J. Shields, a horse and buggy
doctor in the hard coal fields of Pennsylvania,
developed something of world-wide importance—
first aid training. Actually, ways of saving life

were already known, but it often happened that injured persons were left to die from hemorrhage, asphyxiation, or shock, because bystanders did not have the training to use the simple first-aid measures to prevent further injury. What Dr. Shields thought up was a way in which to have everybody adequately trained in first aid.

To those enlightened souls who will wonder why I included the father of first aid and not the father of life saving, the father of parking meters and not the father of traffic lights, the father of basketball and not the father of roller derbies, the father of Labor Day and not the father of Memorial Day, the father of correspondence courses and not the father of manual training schools, the father of the movies and not the father of television, it is only fair to say that I selected the subject of these biographies as I learned about them. There are names of recent times, like Taylor and Magee, against those of men like Battin and Jenkins whom their countrymen have ungratefully forgotten.

Some readers will challenge certain fathers in this book; and I won't blame them. The records of the lives of many fathers look like an enormous palimpsest where different versions appear for the beginning of their masterpieces, each record dating from a different period, each written by a different hand, each giving a different story of events. Many sources contradict each other. I compared all sources of information until the images first of imposters, then of publicity seekers, finally of the fathers loomed through the misty outline.

When I gathered the material for the chapter on Herbert F. Rawll, I thought there was no doubt about his fathering of Christmas Clubs. From my reading of the published stories, I thought that Rawll had done a good piece of work, but, knowing never to stop when I think I have enough, I found Merkel Landis still living in Carlisle, Pa., where the first Christmas Club was started in 1909, and asked him to shed more light on Rawll. According to the old *Literary Digest*, Rawll sold the idea of Christmas Clubs to Landis, then treasurer of a Carlisle bank, and later bought the idea back in order to devote the rest of his life to Christmas Clubs. Landis said that he did not even know Rawll and that he, not Rawll, sponsored the first Christmas Club in America. Then he sold his rights to a Harrisburg banker with whom Rawll was in business. On the other hand, Rawll did so much and Landis so little to spread the movement across the mountains and valleys and plains that I felt justified in thinking of Rawll as the Father of Christmas Clubs; Landis the father of a Christmas Club.

Anyone who has tried to prove that a certain man is worthy of receiving credit for something in which there are disputants will appreciate the daunting nature of this task. It seems that the men who have done the most in the beginning to put new contributions across to the people deserve the credit.

Let me hasten to add that the writing of these biographies was more than a mere salute to individual contributions. I wish to show what new developments, through the men who started them, have meant in the life of this country in various generations and fields of endeavor. The chapters are not as comprehensive as a definitive work, their object being rather to present, within the length of an ordinary magazine article, a selective survey of biographical material, ranging from the forgotten scientist of our age down to the unsung builder of warships of the American Revolution.

Going over my notes, I find random scraps of knowledge from their lives that I had no opportunity to use. Taylor grew a beard to make himself look older than the students in his college classes, although in many cases he was younger. Magee never carried a gun after he accidentally shot one of his friends. Rawll's check books showed checks drawn to "Cash" where the funds were actually given to some needy individual or cause. Naismith, who might have been a minister but for idle curses, was an outstanding football center. McParlan was a streetcar conductor when he tabbed for a career in labor espionage. Jenney's body was cremated. Battin was born a Quaker. Outcault turned his back on newspaper associates when he became rich. Foster spent his youth as a shoe clerk. Cadman nearly lost his life in a mining accident. McGuire, who was once a dangerous radical, is honored among the Catholic dead. Jenkins learned to fly when he was past fifty years of age.

An effort has been made in these pages not only to publish a passable likeness of each father, but also to describe his appearance. Nothing is more persistently demanded in historical research than the color of a man's eyes, his hair, his height, and other physical characteristics. It should be added that any marked variations from the average picture of a man's appearance should be attributed to the scarcity of such material. Above all the deeds of these men whose destiny was larger, if not deeper than our own, attracted me to shake them loose from the cobwebs of archives. Little did they realize the importance of what they were doing.

If I have succeeded in explaining their lives in terms that would enlarge our understanding of their contributions to society, I feel that I have contributed something to the memory of unsung makers of American traits. Cast more sunlight upon them!

EDWARD PINKOWSKI

Philadelphia, Pa.
November, 1953

FORGOTTEN FATHERS

FORGOTTEN FATHERS

FORGOTTEN FATHERS

FORGOTTEN FATHERS

Chapter One

Father of Modern Librarians

The college freshman passed hastily across the threshold of Amherst College Library and climbed a spiral staircase which led to wrought-iron balconies and tiers of books on all sides of the high-ceilinged room.

"Where are you going?" asked the man in charge.

"To look for essay topics," the youth replied.

"Students do not have access to the shelves," the librarian warned. "You must wait at a table until your books are brought to you."

The student from Oneida, a small village in the upper part of New York State, sat down at a long table in the center of the room while the librarian went to look for his material. He was not yet twenty, though his luxuriant black hair and long sideburns, which partially concealed his heavy, projecting jaws, made him appear somewhat older on first view. He looked so fierce that any stage producer of *Faust* wouldn't have hesitated to cast him in the role of Mephistopheles. But *Faust* wasn't on the student's mind. A miser of time, he was appalled at the lack of efficiency and waste of time by the librarian in serving the college students. The books were evidently not always kept in the same place.

Pretty soon he had forgotten the books he wanted, forgotten that he had come to the Massachusetts college to study pedagogy, forgotten everything save the one thing that was to him of the greatest moment—free access to the shelves. He wanted to get at the books himself, and was not content to find them out of reach and subject to shifting and change.

The majority of the 23,000,000 library card holders in the United States may never have heard of him, but Melvil Dewey did more than any other American to make things easier for them. He invented a simple system for numbering and arranging books that is now in use in almost all of the country's 7,400 public libraries, 1,700 college libraries and 1,500 special libraries. His influence changed the library from a bedlam of books to a place of order and source of information. He also created a library school which has done much to put librarians on an equal footing with other professional people.

These two achievements are enough to fill a life. But to understand the father of modern librarians you have to know something about his formative years. Originally named Melville Louis Kossuth Dewey, he was born December 10, 1851, in the crossroads village of Adams Center, New York, and, in his early life, followed the work of his father, who ran a general store and made boots. He had haphazard schooling but early showed a marked eagerness for keeping things in order. He was constantly straightening out his mother's pantry. At sixteen he stood on the platform of a country school and delivered an oration on the intolerable evil of wasting time. The following year he completed an inventory of his father's store in an effort to cut out guess work and learned that his father lost more in charge accounts than his business was worth. He persuaded his father to sell the store, and the family then moved to Oneida.

He probably wouldn't have gone to college if there hadn't been a seminary right there in Oneida to prepare him for it. He chose Amherst because it was, at that time, the only college that required him to spend at least an hour each day in a gymnasium. The setting-up exercise and the Indian clubs that he had learned to use kept him physically fit, and he continued the daily exercises almost to the day of his death. He also went horseback riding every morning except Sunday.

Amherst was then a sleepy and quiet town; a

young student from another state could find little to do there outside his academic studies. Dewey slid through his freshman year, too, without throwing off any sparks. He was an impeccable student, and, discovering the chaos at the college library, he volunteered to help the librarian, William L. Montague, who had originally come to Amherst to teach Latin in 1859.

In his sophomore year this placid existence was shattered by the waste of time in recataloging and reclassifying books in order to provide shelf space for new books. In discussing this problem with Montague, Dewey felt himself to be in a different world from that in which as an 18-year-old preparatory student he learned to save time by using the metric system of weights and measures instead of the bothersome Roman notations. He found the numbering system discouraging; he didn't like the way each book was numbered according to tier and shelf. Yet he could not stop thinking of all the librarians with little skill or experience who woud be faced with the same time-killing problem.

To solve that problem was the main pre-occupation of his junior year when for the first time he was paid $12.50 a month to work in the library. He plunged heart and soul into his studies. One day while he sat in the college chapel, without hearing a word of the president's sermon, he had a proverbial experience. He jumped to his feet and almost shouted "Eureka!" He had a supremely blissful feeling that by using arabic numerals as decimals his worries were over. By dividing the fields of knowledge into ten, by subdividing, then further subdividing, he produced a decimal classification system.

Go into any public library and look around. From 010 to 999 the books are in serried ranks, shelf on top of shelf, marshalled according to Dewey's plan of organization. Each class has a distinguishing number: philosophy, 1; religion, 2; sociology, 3; philology, 4; natural science, 5; useful arts, 6; fine arts, 7; literature, 8; history, 9; cyclopedias and periodicals, 0. Each of these classes is divided into ten divisions, and each division is further subdivided into sections. By adding more numbers, any library can expand the decimal classification system as much as it wants. This book, for instance, is numbered 920.07. The first number immediately indicates that it is history; 2 represents biography, and because this collection of biographies fall in no particular category, the third number is simply 0, and .07 indicates North America.

With this decimal system in mind, the tall, back-haired timesaver from Oneida proceeded to rearrange the books at the Amherst library. When he was in doubt about the classification of a book, he consulted a member of the faculty or visited another library to study its system. He saw at the Boston Athenaeum, for example, that books dealing with horses were grouped under the title of horses and not under zoology. The books which gave him the most trouble concerned Buddhism. It was a religion in India but both a religion and a philosophy in Japan. By the end of that year there was little hope left in the Dewey family that Melvil would turn out to be anything more useful than a librarian.

After graduation, he succeeded Montague as librarian and undertook to prepare a relative subject index as a guide to librarians. Another Amherst graduate of 1874, Walter S. Biscoe, joined him and this period of his life was devoted to a breakdown of all human knowledge into class numbers from 010 to 999. His *Decimal Classification and Relativ Index*, first published as a thin volume of forty-two pages in 1876, was enlarged and revised from time to time. Its thirteen edition, on which he was working at the time of his death, appeared in 1932 with 1,647 pages.

Originally prepared for the world's fair in Philadelphia, the birthplace of the nation a century earlier, the document created a furore in the library world. It seemed, however, the intention of Dewey to do more than that with his decimal system. The year he published the first index, the people of the United States could borrow only 12, 276,964 volumes from 3,647 libraries. The libraries were not free as they are now; they were subscription libraries. There were no school libraries, no children's departments, and last but not least no trained librarians at all.

He went to Boston and, with the financial aid of the Ginn brothers, prepared to launch a business career—the business of library progress. His most important task was to persuade and cajole and nag libraries into giving up their slipshold cataloging methods to accept the decimal system of classification and other standards for greater efficiency.

No sooner had he laid down a plan for a library journal than he heard that a similar project was afoot in New York. He hurried there to confer with the prime movers of the New York project, Frederick Leypoldt and Richard R. Bowker, for whom up to now he wrote library notes which appeared in *Publishers' Weekly*. Dewey yielded to Leypoldt's wish to publish the library journal and cancelled his own arrangements except to edit the publication in Boston. The first

9

number appeared in September, 1876, and was available for a national conference of librarians which Dewey engineered at Philadelphia the next month.

Probably it was Dewey's invention as well as his fanatic, impersonal devotion to library progress that brought 103 librarians, and later an ever-increasing host of adherents, rallying around him. They sensed his indomitable courage, energy, and persistence.

His appearance invited confidence. About five feet, eleven inches tall, weighing about 175 pounds, sturdy and erect, with a strong pair of jaws capable of cracking any nut in the world, he gave evidence that here was one endowed by nature to hold his own against any and all opposition. He dressed meticulously and conservatively. He did not drink, smoke, gamble or swear; his only vice was decimals: he took to 1, 2, and 3 the way other boys took to baseball, and could work a problem in arithmetic in his head quicker than others could on paper. He was too serious to be popular. But when he stood up on a lecture platform his luminous eyes, wells of dark, intelligent light, would shine and he instantly became the man of the hour. No librarian ever carried a more explosive swinging scimitar of words

Although Justin Winsor, Harvard's leonine

librarian, was elected to preside over the first convention of the American Library Association, the persuasive Dewey provided the motive power and for a quarter of a century shaped the policies of the organization. He not only conducted long correspondences with obscure librarians from all over the world, discussing the problems of library work with them as though they were heads of large institutions, but also edited the official organ, *Library Journal,* during the most trying years of the A. L. A. For sixteen years he served as secretary under six different presidents and for three years was president in his own right.

Under him the A. L. A. lived up to its motto: "The best reading for the largest number at the least cost." Those who now thumb through catalog cards and observe short cuts in writing of every sort find it hard to realize that their grandparents did not know such library practices. Just as Dewey spread his decimal classification system, so he introduced standard catalog cards, abbreviations, and an employment agency to find qualified persons for library jobs. By the time he turned over his work in the A. L. A. to younger hands he had accomplished almost the complete standardization of library supplies and equipment.

For a man who was as meticulous about

11

details as Dewey, the illogicalities of English spelling shocked him. He never did follow the spelling of words exactly as Noah Webster did. When he was a child he didn't know better, and when he reached the age of reason he tried as much as possible to practice simplified spelling. In keeping with his gospel, he dropped his middle name and shortened his first name from *Melville* to *Melvil*. Then, as his responsibilities increased in Boston, he changed his surname to *Dui*. The bankers, however, held up his accounts until he went back to the old form. They figured they had to draw the line somewhere in his reform spelling campaign.

At Harvard University, where he went to lecture on his decimal classification system, was a Vassar student named Annie Godrey, who quit college in her junior year to open a library at Wellesley, a liberal arts college for women fifteen miles southwest of Boston. She was a strong-minded girl, an ardent Victorian, and deeply interested in library work. She wanted to know more about Dewey's library scheme. It was good luck that Dewey followed up the lecture with frequent visits to Wellesley. In 1878, the year after their return from London where they had gone to take part in the first international library conference, they were married. Annie shared both the

12

interests and the thoughts of the man she loved. One son was born to them; and Dewey proved to be an attentive and indulgent father. This man, generally high strung and sometimes mercurial, was capable of deep affection and of warm friendships, as, for instance, his long relation with Walter S. Biscoe.

Closely linked to Dewey's love of library economy was his love of attending conventions. One year he left his wife at a convention party to visit a barber shop. As he dozed in the chair, the barber not only cut his hair but also shaved off the beard which he had raised at Amherst in order to hide his pugnaciousness. One of the delegates decided to introduce him to Mrs. Dewey as another person. She extended her hand as though she were happy to meet a new delegate. Suddenly she stopped as she recognized the face.

"If I had ever known that you had a chin like that," she exclaimed, "I never would have married you."

The factor that Dewey's library plans had already gathered momentum in and around Boston enabled him to look for greener pastures to conquer. In 1883, Frederick A. P. Barnard, a scientific man whom Dewey first met when the American Metric Bureau was set up in Boston to advocate the exclusive use of decimal weights

13

and measures, invited him to become the master planner of Columbia University's new library. Dewey accepted on one condition: he would be given a chance to open a library school on the campus.

His career as librarian at Columbia University was as brilliant as it was grief. Thanks to his managerial ability, he gathered together all the books which were scattered in the various departments and college societies and brought six seniors from Wellesley to catalogue and classify them. He created a large reading room for the use of 200 students at a time and engaged assistants to help readers with their problems and when they were culling notes at a table to bring them other books on demand so as to save them time. He met the freshmen class every year and showed them how to use books and consult authorities. The popularity of the library rose rapidly and the number of volumes tripled in five years.

As the years passed, Dewey's idea of establishing a school to teach librarianship took shape. Four subjects which he considered indispensable were bibliography, book buying, reading, and literary methods. The college, however, provided nothing to open the library school except a recitation room—no funds, no teachers, and no equipment. Dewey, whom Bowker called the Edison of

14

the library field, enrolled his own students and arranged other details.

On January 5, 1887, the day the world's first library school was scheduled to open, the college trustees closed the lecture hall to him. The reason was that he had more women than men in his first class. The trustees knew neither the man nor the importance of his idea. A pugnaciousness in propagating his own strongly phrased ideas, a gesture many people considered egotistic, rendered Dewey an opponent. His tall, spare Yankee form stiffened under opposition. His black eyes flashed lightning warnings of intense mental operations.

The mercurial pioneer found a few janitors and led them to a store room over the chapel. They moved out the packing boxes, scrubbed the floor, ran in temporary wires, and set up a number of worn out tables and chairs. Dewey sent a wagon to his home to pick up some more furniture. A janitor was still nailing a broken leg to a table when the first class of 26 students, nineteen of whom were women, gathered in the improvised quarters the following morning. What they lacked in facilities Dewey made up in enthusiasm.

One can well imagine how shocked the trustees were by the petticoat invasion of the Columbia campus, first by the six Wellesley girls and now

15

by nineteen women in the library school. They suspended Dewey and appointed a committee to decide whether or not he should be expelled for admitting women to Columbia. The Amherst graduate of 1874 refused to give up the school, and risked his own professional life in order to train women in a new and remunerative bread-winning pursuit.

During the fight over the library school Whitelaw Reid, influential editor of the New York *Tribune*, asked Dewey for suggestions to improve the State Library at Albany and the New York State Board of Regents, a group which Reid controlled in order to promote his political interests. Reid liked his proposals to expand the State Library and to unify the literary and scientific trustees committed to the Board of Regents.

The School of Library Economy was a flourishing success, but the trustees' continued opposition to women students put an end to it after two years. Dewey resigned in December, 1888, to become State Librarian and Secretary of the New York Board of Regents, and the library school was transferred to Albany five months later.

But the fight was not yet won. It was merely changed to a new battlefield, and it took the unquenchable ardor of the library evangelist to hold his own against unscrupous politicians on the banks of the Hudson. Some members of the Board of Regents were just as much opposed to the library school in the state capitol building as the trustees were at Columbia. They held his budget so low that the assistants he brought with him from Columbia received nothing extra for teaching library science. Even Andrew Carnegie, who set aside a considerable portion of his steel fortune to build public libraries, turned down his appeals to support the training of professional librarians.

Besides the library school, he had a number of other duties, He was, as he observed, "as busy as a cricket on a hot griddle." Under the Regents' jurisdiction he had much to do with New York's institutions of higher learning. One day he received an application for a charter from an institution known as "The College for the Training of Teachers for the City of New York." He grunted at the number of superfluous words in the title. He asked the college authorities to change the name to "Teachers' College," and then issued a new charter. While on this job, he simplified the spelling of many words in school textbooks. *Ghospel, fyshe, academical* and many other spellings have now become obsolete.

His eleven years as secretary of the Board of

Regents were more hectic than the five preceeding years at Columbia. He moved so fast that he had his fingers in another pie before the politicians could digest the first one. He met political opposition at every turn of the way, yet he advanced in whatever he set out to do. He advanced the program of state aid to education. He juggled legislative appropriations around to provide funds for traveling libraries not only unauthorized but definitely forbidden. One of his associates remarked, "He would venture out on a gossamer thread and always land."

For six years after resigning as the Board's secretary, he continued as State Librarian and Director of the Library School. Although politicians scorned him, librarians felt at ease in his presence. In fact, Mr. and Mrs. Dewey had many devoted friends who filled the household for teas, dinners, and weekend visits. Mrs. Dewey, who was a bright, graceful woman, looked like a butterfly as she moved about in her flowerly dresses, but she suffered with June rose cold trouble as her husband did with autumnal hey fever. For the last forty years of her life, from 1882 to 1922, they searched for a place where they would be immune from these afflictions.

In the early days of their sojourn in Albany, they found relief in the pure air of the Adirondack mountains around Lake Placid. The couple established their summer home and had not been long at Lake Placid before Dewey had another idea. In all his years with the library movement he had not known many librarians who could afford to take vacations. So he decided to launch a summer resort at Lake Placid where those devoted to education—librarians and social workers, teachers and preachers—could receive, at moderate cost, the rest and recreation they needed.

Dewey's long life was a spectacle of unwavering devotion to library work. This was dramatically illustrated when his enemies, in their attacks on the library school at Albany, discovered that he was the author of the *Decimal Classification and Relativ Index* used by the library students. They charged him with malfeasance in office. Dewey took the stand in his own defense. He punctured the attacks upon him by proving that he gave the various editions of the library aid to the students at his own expense.

His enemies, of course, were dedicated to liquidate him. They merged his functions with other educational activities under Dr. Andrew S. Draper, with whom Dewey came to grips several years earlier. Dewey realized that one department wasn't large enough to hold the former

19

superintendent of public instruction and himself. Their personalities were too strong. He resigned in 1905 and devoted the rest of his life to the anti-Semitic Lake Placid Club. Now that he made it his all-year-round residence, Lake Placid Club remained open in the winter as well as in the summer.

Dewey never lost his interest in library work. As new inventions were introduced and described in books, he picked out new decimal numbers and listed the new subjects in new editions of his major work. Librarians often came to consult with him. One of them enjoying telling how one day a new word came up in the discussion and, the dictionary being in another room, he dashed from the dining room, his napkin sailing from his vest, fountain pens visible in his vest pocket, to learn the meaning of the word in his favorite Funk and Wagnalls unabridged dictionary.

He sent out hundreds of men and women, imbued with his own eagerness and enthusiasm, to spread the gospel of librarianship to every corner of the world. They carried his library methods across the rivers and lakes, mountains and prairies, and into many foreign countries. In 1926, when the library school was moved back to Columbia, Dewey found that out of 1,400 graduates at Albany most of them were taking a lead-

ing part in opening new libraries. Six were head
of library schools founded on the same pattern as
Dewey's and several were on the faculties of
eight others.

Even his indomitable spirit, however, could
not for long keep up with the activities of his
graduates. Two decades after establishing Lake
Placid Club he set up a counterpart in Florida.
Spending the summers in New York and the
winters in Florida strengthened his spirit but not
his vitality. He died on December 25, 1931, in his
eighty-first year.

Library chaos gradually disappeared from
our public libraries, and to Dewey's *Decimal
Classification and Relativ Index* and library
methods America owes its remarkable uniformity
of library economy. No other man did so much to
save the time of librarians. No other man did so
much to produce them. And today about 30,000
trained librarians, 90 percent of them women,
bear testimony to Melvil Dewey's labors and superb genius.

Chapter Two

Father of Modern Radar

One blistering day in the summer of 1922, Dr. A. Hoyt Taylor, a rawboned, sandy-haired physicist, put a bizarre radio receiver on the back seat of his old Dodge touring car and drove across the Anacostia River to the tongue of grassy land lying between it and the Potomac. With him to operate the set was a short, dark-haired assistant named Leo Young. The willow trees that outlined Haines Point shielded signals from a transmitter at Anacostia air station, and the two experimenters moved the receiver from the car to the edge of a sea wall.

The signals were clearer, but suddenly, instead of clear signals, they heard beat notes as if someone were plucking two piano strings. At first they were annoyed, then excited, when Taylor saw a mile or so away an excursion boat coming up the river toward Washington, D. C.

The beat notes grew louder as the ship came closer. Both men, who were engaged in developing a short wave radio set to replace blinker lights for the Navy, were quick to grasp the meaning of the fluctuating signals. Never until that moment had it been known that radio waves could be reflected from small moving objects as definitely as from mountains and buildings.

The outcome of their discovery was radar. More than any other man, Dr. Taylor guided radar, which is now a billion-dollar industry, into existence as the most versatile weapon of the war. It enabled bombardiers to reach their targets and hit them accurately by providing a magic eye to see through darkness, fog, smoke and rain. It came out of the war as the all-seeing eye, and scientists have found thousands of peacetime uses for radar.

Dr. Albert Hoyt Taylor is now watching the hero of wondrous war feats and servant of civilian gadgets from a neat little bungalow in Claremont, California. He still stands, a little hunched, to his full height of five feet and ten inches and tips the scales, as he has for the last forty years, at 150 pounds. He has mild blue eyes and a broad fringe of white hair around the back of a bald-domed head. His white toothbrushlike mustache and restrained bantering manner, and his speech, as wholesome as the wheat of his beloved Dakotas, gives the impression of an ascetic troubleshooter on a holiday. Few descriptions have appeared of him, but none fits him so well, he feels, as his own: "I am a curious cross between a physicist, an inventor, a naval officer and a radio engineer."

To these faculties he grafts a small shoot of the philosopher and the college lecturer. He indulges in a curve-stemmed pipe while he talks or writes, putting on and removing horn-rimmed glasses and staring into space. He lights the pipe constantly, either with matches or a cigarette lighter, and unless someone is around to offer him a lighter, he smokes matches instead of tobacco.

Until he retired a few years ago, he directed the radio division of the Naval Research Laboratory, on the muddy flats of the Potomac near Washington, for twenty-two years. Under him the division grew, through off-phase years, from 23 to 1000 persons. Under him they conducted thousands of investigations and produced an amazing number of devices, some of which are still secret. The shrewd, imaginative physicist's own achievements in radio, which has helped to make the Navy research-minded, made him during the war the Navy's top civilian scientist.

If you had visited his office then, you would have imagined you were in a lecture hall. Invariably he dictated on his feet, striding restlessly back and forth across the floor of his handsome office, and his words flowed smoothly and precisely in a calm, low voice. If he wanted to be emphatic, he lapsed into German, but his secretary did not take it down. She figured you had to draw the line somewhere.

Yet, in 1922, when he solved the problem of magic echoes on a mossy sea wall in the shadow of the Washington Monument, only a handful of people understood the far-away look in Taylor's eyes. Quickly he set down in writing the evidence that showed what he could do with the radio equipment at sea. In a seven-page letter he requested permission to do simply this: to put certain equipment on a number of destroyers, take them out to sea at night, and prove that other ships could not move between the destroyers without detection. But this important letter, down to a picture of possible war-time uses of radio detection, came to naught.

Taylor's vision didn't, though. He realized that the detection of moving objects by radio held the promise of a new kind of life. He stuck with it. His first chance came in 1923, with the establishment of the Naval Research Laboratory, in which the Navy put all its research groups. As superintendent of the radio division, he surrounded himself with a bunch of young servicemen who had served under him during World War I.

Two of these veterans were Leo C. Young and Louis G. Gebhard. Both were crazy about radio and loyal to Doctor Taylor. Young, a shy fellow with studious cat's eyes set close to a short hawklike nose, twelve years younger than Taylor, had neither time nor inclination for anything else. Like Young, tall, blue-eyed Gebhard, now fifty-nine, robbed King Morpheus of the greatest part of many nights trying to solve a problem Taylor had given him.

Two years after Taylor got started in this project, Gebhard produced the first radio transmitter using the electronic "pulse" principle. With two other physicists Young built a receiver to pick up the reflected waves of Gebhard's transmitter. Together they used the equipment to explore the ionosphere, sometimes called the Kennelly-Heaviside layer, which is the body of electrically charged particles surrounding the earth's outer atmosphere. They measured the height of this layer by bouncing radio waves off it and catching their echo on a receiver.

The upshot of Taylor's dream was memorable. On June 24, 1930, Taylor, Young, and another assistant, Lawrence A. Hyland, a serious, hot-tempered Irishman, were testing a short-wave landing system for aircraft when they ran into trouble. Hyland was not getting clear signals from the transmitter Young had in another corner of the field where they were testing. Hyland began checking his equipment, but he found nothing wrong with the receiver. Suddenly he heard a plane in the distance and noticed the interference again. It happened every time a plane passed overhead and he ran to report it to Taylor and Young.

"We all got pretty excited," Taylor recalled. "We knew that anything which could detect plane would be of enormous importance in defense."

In January, 1931, the Navy finally decided to "investigate use of radio to detect the presence of enemy vessels and aircraft." But unfortunately the decision carried no bank roll. Doctor Taylor had to take funds from other research projects to pay expenses.

His men worked on aircraft detection for several months. They used various frequencies to bounce waves off planes and detected their presence as far as forty miles away. Then, because the devices for sending and receiving radio waves were too bulky, he suggested that the Army use the equipment for the defense of cities, and he sought more compact devices for ships and planes.

Before starting on something new, he usually acted like an octopus. He grabbed in every direction and carefully studied his target. When he found something worthwhile, he called in his assistants and, thinking aloud, outlined its general pattern. The discussion that generally followed helped him to marshall his thoughts in an orderly manner. That's what he did with the problem of clumsy apparatus, and his sounding board was no less an inventive genius than Young.

One day the ex-telegrapher from Illinois walked into Dr. Taylor's office with a hopeful gleam behind his gold-rimmed glasses. "Remember the Kennelly-Heaviside experiments?" he asked. "Why don't we do this thing with pulses?"

Well," Taylor replied, "it's a long way up there to the ionosphere. That gives you a long time-interval between emission of the pulse and its reception, which is probably why the pulse worked so well in those experiments. I doubt whether it would work on shipboard, considering the compact apparatus and the short distances we must work with there. Go ahead, however, and see what you can do."

After months of inspired research, Young invented the pulse system of plane detection, now the heart of radar, and no one patted him on the back more than his able, self-effacing boss. After that they sat down to design other machines to show the position, angle and speed of a distant plane or ship.

Then came a crushing blow. In 1934, in the middle of the depression, only $165,000, as compared with millions during the war, was available for all research projects, and radar was singled out for this comment: "a priority B research problem; expenditures should be held down." And the Navy's chief physicist — never as skilled at finance as he was at invention — lost interest in bookkeeping.

He paced the floor impatiently envisioning the rich promise of radar and then, in spite of little support from the Navy and Congress, he refused to drop the research. He assigned some of his promising young physicists to work with Young on a full-time basis and intensified his efforts to convince the powers above him of his radar's value.

"Radio eyes to see through fog, darkness or smoke screen?" pessimists laughed. "Nonsense!

Taylor must think he is a hoot owl." But, despite such pessimism, the event that catapulted this electronic miracle into top-drawer thinking took place one Sunday in 1935, when Taylor and two associates discussed their needs with the late James Scrugham, an influential member of Congress at the time, in his office. As a result they received $100,000 from Congress to further their investigations.

Promoting radar is a job from which scientists might have shied away. But not Dr. Taylor. He became a salesman par excellence. Top-ranking admirals and key Congressmen were invited — not once, but many times — to see the radar work being done at the Naval Research Laboratory, and always present was the white-haired father of the weapon with a few choice words in the right places. His work was still not tried at sea. Finally, in 1936, the Navy decided to give it a chance at sea, and the first use of the equipment detected destroyers at a range of eight miles. It was not until two years later that the first entirely successful radar set was installed aboard a Navy vessel.

From the realization of his 16-year-old dream you might think of Dr. Taylor as having reached the height of professional pride. Actually he was in a dither about something else.

Shortly before Munich, in 1938, Dr. Taylor, in reading German newspapers which his son, then studying in Germany, had sent him, discovered a mood of war overhanging Germany. He worked harder than ever to get radar into production and to the ships of the line at the earliest possible moment.

He was also immersed in the enormous task of getting scientists and technicians for the vast research and development ahead. For many of his young researchers, he had to go to the colleges and universities. Slowly and by example Taylor played a great influence on their careers. He got along well with untried, temperamental scientists because he put them where they liked to work and could do their best. But there was the iron hand underneath his gentle approach that he used with indomitable strength and courage when necessary. But first, with a personal appeal and persuasion, he got results.

Yet people wonder how he managed to keep two diverse functions — science and administration — from tangling. He set both side by side without either getting in his way. The answer is that he had a unique organization in which both functions were built around his abilities. His type of organization could not have succeeded unless he were running it. When he retired from his administrative duties, for example, his organization was split into four divisions.

He succeeded because he was shrewd, gifted, and a many-sided leader who begot tremendous loyalty from his men. The quality that associates most admired in him was his fairness. He asked an individual to assume responsibility in accordance with his capabilities. Not only did he teach men the art of responsibility, but he also gave them credit for whatever they did well. This trait effectively welded a strong bond and real understanding between Taylor and his workers. Very few who had ever worked for him ever left him.

"A man of his standing," said Raymond B. Meyer, who was superintendent of the transmitter section at the Naval Research Laboratory, "could mold your future better than you could yourself." Meyer should know, for as Taylor's yoeman during the first World War Dr. Taylor steered him from the food brokerage business, which he had planned to enter after the war, to the more promising field of electronics. Dr. Taylor kept telling him, "You've got to go out and become a radio engineer."

"But I don't know anything about radio."

"Sure, you do," Taylor said. "You know more about radio than you think you do. Now go out and take the examination for radio laboratorian."

With the coaching of Young and Gebhard, who had earlier taken the Civil Service exams for this position, Meyer was able to get a higher grade than either of his coaches.

Harking back to his youth, Taylor cannot remember ever having any ambition other than to be an inventor. The only child of elderly parents from New England, he was born in Chicago the first day of 1879. As a boy, in a suberb north of the Windy City called Wilmette, he built a carbon arc, an induction coil and even a telegraph line with 88 parties on it.

At Northwestern University, he attracted the special attention of the head of the physics department, a tall, spare, militant Quaker named Henry Crew, when he developed his own version of Hertzian waves. Professor Crew taught the laboratory upstart that if he wanted to become a scientist he'd have to set high standards for himself. He instilled in the student from Wilmette a desire to do real research in wireless telegraphy.

But there was doubt whether he would get his sheepskin. He had started college on a few dollars scraped from the family budget. He worked his way up through the third year by installing electric door bells and burglar alarms in new houses. Then he left college and found a job in a Western Electric shop in Chicago. His aunt heard of his predicament and sent him enough money to go back to Northwestern for one semester, but he had to look for work again. Professor Crew stepped in and got him a job teaching physics at Michigan State College of Agriculture in Lansing. There, along with some of his students, he won his B. S. degree in 1902.

After that he had more time to devote to science. To present models for his classes, he worked at night making them in the college laboratory. His endless experiments in radio irritated a number of people, and one day the college president reprimanded him for wasting his time on strange noises. Taylor left, therefore, to teach physics at the University of Wisconsin in Madison.

The head of his department tried to discourage him from wireless telegraphy, but Taylor insisted on it, and all but moved his bed into the laboratory. Another professor encouraged him to study precise electrical measurements in order to further his investigations.

As early as this Taylor's dream was to develop very high frequencies, build sets for transmitting and receiving them, and then — and this is the engineering ability in him — turn them into practical uses. But his hunger for knowledge was still not satisfied.

"Where do you think I should go?" he asked Professor Crew.

"Taylor," he said, "what you need is to study spiritualized electrical engineering."

For that reason he went to the University of Goettingen in Germany on a scholarship. Upon getting his degree, *cum laude*, Taylor served as head of the physics department for twelve years at the University of North Dakota in Grand Forks. In 1911, on the strength of his university job, he married Sarah E. Hickman, a small attractive woman he had known since his first day in Grand Forks. She was the university's head librarian. Four children—one boy and three girls — were born of this union.

An experimenter at heart, he worked in his spare time to make headway in his studies of wave propogation. He reached radio hams for miles around, and learned from them the results of his work in short waves. He also grounded his students well in physics and the theories of wave propagation. "Radio is a great new frontier," he would say on the lecture platform and then demonstrated its potentialities in his own pursuits.

He was also beginning to attract attention in national radio circles. When, at thirty-eight, he was in New York to deliver a paper on radio transmission phenomena, he met Rear Admiral William H. G. Bullard, the first director of naval communications, and arranged to hook up his experimental station with the Navy's at Great Lakes, Illinois. But his call signal, 9KN, soon went off the air. None of his radio hams knew what had happened.

Suddenly, in April, 1917, thousands of them in the Ninth, Tenth, and Eleventh Naval Districts were stunned. Their 4-KW operator from Grand Forks was in a Navy lieutenant's uniform at Great Lakes. They were stunned because his first job was to close all the amateur radio stations and to send Navy radio operators to run the commercial stations in the three Midwestern districts.

Many radio amateurs, however, turned around and tramped to Taylor's headquarters. Could he use them in the war effort? Yes, he could. Simultaneously the Navy asked him to conduct experiments to improve the reception of trans-Atlantic messages. He began his basic research with a handful of men working from a tent on the windy shores of Lake Michigan.

Little by little the work went forward. With satisfactory equipment, Taylor took the team to the nerve center of trans-Atlantic communications at Belmar, New Jersey, to install and run the machinery. As commanding officer of that center, Taylor learned that anything can happen.

For many days his men lived in cold barracks. Taylor used up all the fuel—coal, wood, and kerosene — he could find in the neighborhood, but it wasn't enough to last through the cold spell. His temper reached the boiling point. Every day he called the local freight master to see whether the 600 tons of coal Washington ordered had come in. Finally, when the coal arrived, the station master told him when he called: "You can't get it, because the Bill of Lading hasn't arrived."

"Look here," Taylor said, "the railroad is in the hands of the government and I am working for the government. Will you give me that coal, or do I have to send the Marines to get it?"

Shortly after the coal arrived, Taylor was ordered to Norfolk Air Station, where Pat Bellinger, who was then commanding officer of the station, asked him to organize an experimental division in aircraft radio work. And Bellinger pitch-forked him, as Taylor says, into the task when, Taylor protesting that he knew nothing about aviation, he said: "Oh, that's all right. Go out, hunt up a pilot, and get a hop."

The point was reached where, without proper equipment, he was assigned to organize an aircraft radio laboratory in Washington, D.C., and his old reliables, members of his original research team and others discovered along the way, plunged into the work with him. It was a different laboratory from the radio room at Grand Forks or the hectic, wartime atmosphere of Belmar. But Taylor took it amazingly well. Instead of college students, he had a group of young servicemen who wanted to continue working under him. They were encouraged to apply for Civil Service positions just before discharge.

After the war Taylor had a tussle with himself to decide whether to return to the lecture hall or remain in Naval research. At forty-four, he felt that he had just reached his prime. As he lay in a Washington hospital, where he was fighting against a rotten appendix, he pondered his future. The Navy had left a deep imprint on him. So he accepted a position as Expert Radio Aide, at a salary of $5,000 a year, a position which was specially created for his talents.

But the Civil Service Commission had no one qualified to examine him for this position. Neither had the Navy's Bureau of Engineering — now Bureau of Ships — but the head of the radio division in that bureau asked Dr. Taylor to make up the questions for his own examination.

No sooner had he composed thirty questions than the Bureau of Engineering forwarded them to the Civil Service Commission. A few days later the same questions were sent to Dr. Taylor with a request that he answer them by letter. He did, and the Civil Service Commission graded his papers. His final mark was eighty-nine!

In 1923, when he was made NRL's superintendent of the radio division, Dr. Taylor bought a 10-room house on Pennsylvania Avenue. Every year, in an old hunting rig and a shapeless cap, he trimmed the trees surrounding the home until he sold the place and moved to California.

The way he diverted his mind from the strain of war work helps to explain his enthusiasm in his activities. Since his college days, he has continued to read German and French and, occasionally, Spanish literature. He speaks some of each, and is very fluent in German. For many years he briefed his staff on articles in foreign technical publications, and in that way kept them abreast with developments in Europe. In the late twenties an Italian scientist, Adriano C. Ducati, sent him a copy of a book entitled "Le onde Corte," in which Taylor's work in short waves was discussed in Italian. It made Taylor so inquisitive that he studied Italian until he could read the book and other Italian publications. Lately he has added his sixth language, Russian, to his linguistic ledger.

His greatest triumph, however, came in 1945 when he was awarded the U. S. Medal of Merit for his work in radar. It was one of the first medals given for distinguished civilian service in World War II. He is the only man living who has won this distinguished honor together with the Medal of Honor from the Institute of Radio Engineers and the famous John Scott Medal.

In former years, until he triumphed with radar and turned it over to an increasing number of scientists, he worked late, frequently to sunrise, with radio hams in the interest of his projects. As a result he was, and still is, a hard man to get up in the morning. Very seldom, except during the war, did he reach his office until 9:30 or 10 o'clock in the morning.

But he didn't milk the Government. He was his own timekeeper. His habit cost him in the neighborhood of $2,000 a year from his $10,000 salary. But for a Government worker — who, incidentally, had more success with short waves at night on his own time than on the Government's time — this was the rarest and most precious privilege on earth.

Chapter Three

Father of Christmas Clubs

One day in 1910, as Herbert F. Rawll dropped into a Harrisburg, Pennsylvania, bank with his company's line of loose-leaf accounting blanks and binders, the bank president turned from his morning mail to greet him. With his great curly-haired dome of a head and a square, heroic face, Rawll was not solemn, but had a winning smile and a free and easy manner which invited everybody to come to him and be friends.

"You're just the man I want to see," said Charles S. Boll, the bank president. "You're a business efficiency expert, aren't you?"

The energetic salesman with burning hazel eyes admitted he'd been something of the sort for the past ten years. At least, the Harrisburg City Directory listed him as a consulting accountant.

"There's a young factory worker," the banker continued, "who deposits part of her wages in a Carlisle bank every Saturday and she does the the same for other workers who don't have the time to come to the bank themselves. Last Christmas she made out checks to them for the amount of money she deposited for them during the year.

Now with the cashier of the Carlisle bank I want to organize a Christmas Club Savings Company, but I need someone to design various forms to handle the weekly deposits."

The twenty-eight-year-old salesman of Baker-Vawter Company ran his hands through his russet curls. He loved banking and loved to solve banker's problems, but he also hated to do anything unless he saw a purpose behind it. He asked the square-faced bank president for more information and left with a promise that he would see what he could do.

As he worked on the problem of finding a simple accounting system, Rawll learned more about the Carlisle experiment. Quiet shady Colonial houses and dull gray walls of college buildings camouflaged a bustling industrial city, 18 miles west of Harrisburg, and most of its 12,000 citizens worked in factories manufacturing shoes, paper boxes, hosiery, carpets and rugs, and silk goods. One of the shoe workers created a problem which led to one of the most dramatic and noteworthy achievements in America since the turn of the century. She started the ball rolling when she walked into the Carlisle Trust Company, a small bank cater-cornered from the Public Square, and asked Merkel Landis, the 34-year-old cashier, if she could start a savings account

46

early in the year and withdraw the balance just before Christmas.

If she had gone to one of the town's three other banks, she might have had difficulty, But Landis, who had started the bank on a shoestring only four years before, did not object. The girl deposited for herself and others in the mill one cent the first week, two the second week, and so on up to half a dollar in the fiftieth week. After the first Christmas checks were made out, Landis dropped the progressive method of depositing and established a regular weekly amount.

To meet the new system, Rawll originated a sheet of fifty coupons, most of which were in two cent denominations, and passed them along. Older and more prosperous banks in Cumberland Valley immediately nicknamed Carlisle Trust the "two-cent bank." But Landis didn't care. The idea of Christmas money was a wonderful stimulus to business. Within a few years the bank rented the space next door occupied by a jewelry store and expanded considerably. Business grew so heavy that Landis, stuck in the teller's cage on many occasions, had little time to devote to the Landis Christmas Club Savings Company that he had organized with Charles Boll.

Rawll, however, forgot about the Christmas Club idea until W. A. Vawter, president of

Baker-Vawter, sent for him to come to the company's headquarters in Chicago. "Herbert," said Vawter, "do you know what your commissions were this year?" Rawll's mind raced back to the day in 1899, the year he started working for the company, when he insisted on a straight commission on sales of the company's products. "One of us has to go out of business," concluded Vawter.

With the last of his commissions from Baker-Vawter in his pocket, Rawll returned to Harrisburg and went to work for the Landis Christmas Savings Plan. He opened a small office, not far from the noisy halls of the State Capitol, and amazed his colleagues with a lot of pep and go. Within a year he brought fifty banks under the new plan.

Landis sold his stock in the company in 1913, and Rawll found himself occupying a key position. But Herb, as all his friends called him, grew more and more restless in Harrisburg and he finally moved his office to Hudson Street, in New York's financial district. He felt that he had to be close to the financial pillars of society to give full play to his aggressiveness. Probably the most remarkable thing about his high nervous-energy potential was that, despite the hair-trigger speed of his reactions, he changed the minds of bankers without making enemies.

One of the first banks where he went to outline his Christmas Club plan was in Mount Vernon, New York. As he advanced his idea in a fast, fluent voice, the chairman of the board of directors sprang to his feet. "Young man," he began, "our bank has stood on the same corner for sixty years as an escutcheon of dignity and a Gibraltar of conservatism. Your five-cent, nickelodeon, trading stamp proposition would make us the laughing stock of the community."

But Rawll asked the annoyed executive if he was connected with a certain church down the street. The banker proudly pointed out that he was an elder in that church, but "I don't see what that has to do with your proposition." "It has plenty," Rawll retorted. "I noticed as I was driving into town that it has a large electric sign, 'Come to Worship.' If a house of God advertises to promote worship," he argued, "why can't a bank advertise to promote thrift, which is certainly a Godly virtue?"

As a result the Mount Vernon Trust Company became the first bank in New York State to adopt the Christmas Club plan. Others quickly followed. The Christmas Clubs Rawll introduced were different from other organizations. They elected no officers, held no meetings, carried on no mutual undertakings. Their membership consisted, as they still do, of individuals who agree to deposit a certain amount in a Christmas Club account.

Out of all this activity Rawll emerged with a banking service organization known as Christmas Club to supply banks with coupon books, punch cards, or bank books with date and amount already printed in them to help provident week-to-week savers select the class of payments best suited to their individual requirements.

Though he was a salesman of many parts, some of them prosaic, the principal target of this new apostle of thrift was spreading Christmas Clubs in the United States. He understood that banks could not grow unless they attracted new depositors, and he convinced bankers that in his Christmas Club he had an ingenuous device to attract new capital for their banks. By the time of the bank holiday in 1933 he installed his system of saving into more than 8,000 banks.

Rawll, who was as statistical-minded as a tabulating machine, made annual surveys to see how many customers he brought into the banks and what they did with their Christmas Club funds. The year he took up the nation's Christmas finances, 16,800,000 persons were depositing money in savings accounts all over the nation. Today there are over 72,000,000 savings accounts. Many believe the use of Christmas Clubs is largely responsible for the tremendous increase in permanent savings accounts.

Out of $831,000,000 distributed to 10,175,000 Christmas Club members in 1948, for example, only 38 per cent of it was used for Christmas gifts. About 32 per cent went back into permanent savings, 8 per cent into insurance payments, 12 per cent for year-end bills, 6 per cent for taxes, and 4 per cent for debt retirement and miscellaneous items. When Rawll first learned that depositors did not spend all of their Christmas funds for gifts, he set up vacation and tax clubs. But they have not prospered as well as Christmas clubs. In 1949 alone there was a growth in Christmas Club membership of 500,000.

In private life, Rawll was as eager to fulfill an obligation as he was in business. Shortly after the war's end in 1918, he met a winsome blonde named Rita Elliott, whose brother, William Elliott, was a well-known Broadway actor and producer. It was on a blind date. Actually, he was on his way to a charity ball in one of New York City's large hotels when William Jefferson, son of the famous actor, dated him with Miss Elliott and took another girl for himself. In keeping with the pattern of his life, Rawll apologized profusely for staying briefly and remarked to Miss Elliott, his eyes swimming with sincerity, "I'd like to give you a party to continue this one." As he set the date and place and got up to go, he added, "Invite as many people as you like."

When Jefferson asked Rita Elliott how she liked Rawll, she remarked, "He is a charming fellow and either the most sincere man I have ever met or he is a brag."

She invited fifty of her friends, and on the night of the party at Sherry's, a gaudy night spot on 44th Street, just off Fifth Avenue, she was surprised to find that Rawll had also invited a number of his friends, including Fay Bainter, the actress.

"I found that I had a rival on my first night," Rita Elliott, whom Rawll married on October 4, 1919, told friends afterwards. "In this case he had assumed the obligation as host to a small party which by reason of another engagement he seemed unable to complete. To show his sincerity and good will he made a gesture so magnanimous that he could have been misunderstood. The whole pattern of his life followed in the direction of seemingly exaggerated statements that he always accomplished."

The Rawlls spent their social evenings with other executives and their wives. He was punctual on dinner dates, and never could adjust himself to the habits of New Yorkers who generally turned up late for various affairs. Often he did vast amounts of research at night to keep abreast of banking and business trends, and sometimes regretted that he did not see enough of his country home in Greenwich, Connecticut.

One spring he decided to spend more time at home. He and his brother-in-law planted a bed of peonies in the garden. For the next few weeks, before heading for the 7:10 commuters' special, he went out to examine the bed and finally demanded, "Where are the peonies?" The gardener dug up the bed and found that the peonies had been planted upside down. That cured the banking service expert of gardening.

He was often described as a Christmas Club Santa. He tried to reach everbody with his "paid for Christmas" plan, and in his well-organized mind he kept a mental record of the spending habits of Christmas Clubbers and was very much interested in their progress. Whenever he walked briskly into a bank to find out about its Christmas Club, he usually came out with new ideas for improving the service. He carried envelopes in his inside coat pocket and noted on them the things he wanted to do. He also went to sleep with a Christmas Club envelope near his bedside, and when he got an idea at night, he'd say, "Well, jot this down. I don't want to forget it."

He inherited his love of statistics from his father, George Rawll, who was in the loose-leaf ledger business in London, England, where Herbert was born on May 31, 1881. When Herb was eight, the family came to the United States and settled in Chicago. There young Rawll went to school. Upon graduation from Lake View High School, he enrolled in Northwestern University but contacted typhoid when the semester began and dropped out. He joined Baker-Vawter and was sent to Pennsylvania to sell and install business accounting services.

Finding a purpose in every enterprise also emerged in his early years. When he was fourteen, he saw a $100 set of Limoges chinaware that he wanted to get for his mother. He cut lawns, carried wood, and delivered messages until he had enough money to buy the set. Nothing was too high for him. He liked to do things in a big way, and always with a noble purpose.

During the first World War, the mastermind of installment saving found an intimate knowledge of business accounting and banking services invaluable. It was important in devising a system of selling $700,000,000 in Liberty Bonds to 15,000,000 subscribers on the partial payment plan.

He waived exemption in 1918, and saw duty in the Army Air Forces, serving as an aviator at several home bases. About this time he also showed a cooperative organization of citizens, widely described as the Community Chest, how to raise funds, by community-wide appeal, for social welfare and health agencies and how to distribute the funds in accordance with a budget procedure.

After the Armistice, he returned to his Christmas Club business only to find that many of his old salesmen had started a similar business of their own. To survive, Rawll drove hard bargains. Where his more cautious competitors sold supplies outright to the banks, Rawll operated on a commission basis, being paid a percentage of Christmas Club deposits.

Far too many people felt that a bank was a rich man's club. Rawll found out that the average individual of small means did not know a great deal about banks or about their functions and and services. No man perhaps did more to humanize banking than the founder of Christmas Club.

In all his advertising, in local newspapers, national magazines, and on the radio, he stressed the value of putting so small an amount as one dollar into a Christmas Club account. Once a person joined a Christmas Club, he visited the bank not once, but nearly fifty times a year. Naturally he also thought of the bank when he wanted to make an investment, open a checking or savings account, secure a safety-vault box, or send a remittance abroad. Rawll arranged with banks, as soon as checks were mailed in December, to send members reminders that they could use part of their Christmas Club savings to open a regular savings account. For his pains thousands of banks established miniature universities of thrift.

The Bank of America, A. F. Giannini's financial wonder in California, has more Christmas Club members than any other bank in the country. Giannini, who had a franchise to use Rawll's services, depended on such deposits as Christmas Clubs provided for his opening of 504 branches in 313 communities.

At first only one bank in an area had the right to buy copyrighted supplies from Rawll to put the Christmas Club service into operation. When the idea became so popular that other banks in the same area wanted the same services, Rawll discarded exclusive rights and established two and more clubs in the same town. As a result some banks cancelled their contracts.

Rawll tried to win them back by making personal visits. One New England banker, however, was adamant. "I'll never renew my contract," he snapped. Rawll went back to see the stubborn executive again the following year and the year after that. Each time the Yankee was as stubborn as the first time.

"Herbert," his wife advised, "why waste your time? You'll never get that man back as a customer."

"Oh, yes, I will," Rawll replied. Some years afterward, when Rawll's car showed plenty of extra mileage, he finally managed to convince the banker that it was to his best interest to renew the contract.

The highly strung human dynamo from England also had his charities and benefactions. It gave him the greatest pleasure to gratify the wishes of others, but he never gave a check in order to show income tax collectors what he gave to charity. Childless themselves, the Rawlls took under their protection the two children left by the death of William Elliott in 1932.

The same year the salesman of Christmas savings decided to extend the Christmas Club idea to retail stores. Under his plan merchants were to issue to customers a certificate on each twenty-five-cent purchase and at the same time deposit the face value of the certificate in a special ac-

count in the bank. Just before Christmas, the
holders of savings certificates were to forward
them to the Christmas Club for redemption, but
the curtailed pay-rolls in industrial centers and
runs on banks seriously hampered its growth.
The plan was dropped until recently when
Rawll's corporation renewed the drive to install
the idea through independent quality stores. Included in the plan for Christmas Club thrifties
is a two per cent dividend on cash sales.

At the beginning of the second World War
Rawll introduced Victory Clubs in banks
throughout the nation. Its members pledged to
use the money saved in one year for War Savings
Bonds. In 1942, a typical year, they used about
12 per cent of the $410,000,000 Christmas Club
fund for the purchase of war bonds.

After working hard to promote Victory Clubs
during the war, Rawll was suddenly struck with
illness. He hardly felt like bending over a desk
on the seventeenth floor of 341 Madison Avenue
to renew his idea of Christmas Club thrifties.
Then complications arose and he was taken to
Greenwich Hospital, but it was too late.

Rawll had so organized his business and
trained his assistants that after his death in 1946
Christmas Club, Inc. carried on with remarkable
efficiency. The board of directors fell back upon

its chairman, Douglas T. Johnston, head of a separate bank service business to fill in the gap, but the pressure of his own business became so great that in March, 1949, he gave way to Edward [F. Dorset, an up and coming executive from Virginia who joined the organization in 1939.

Shortly after Rawll's death, his widow entered actively into the business and devoted much of her time to the Herbert F. Rawll Memorial Awards Competition, offering a total of $5,000 in cash awards for the best human interest stories on the subject: "How the Christmas Club Has Helped Me." The club's filing cabinets are full of letters telling how members were able to start a business, pay off their debts at a crucial moment of their lives, engage surgeons for much needed operations, and improve their homes.

A not-so-usual story of Christmas Club savings is that of a woman in New York's Lower East Side who started a small account in a club some years ago. Each year she rejoined it. She now has a thriving wholesale florist business. Another person, as a result of his Christmas Club savings, is a big real estate man in New England. If they did not first join a Christmas Club with these businesses in view, they at least joined with a purpose in mind — the "smile checks" in their mail boxes during the holiday season.

That is what Rawll put across in his advertising campaigns for affiliated banks. As one banker put it, "We can talk thrift, poverty, security and the like until we're blue in the face — but along comes a pleasant phrase — Christmas Club money — and that gets 'em. Gets 'em by the hundreds and thousands."

Rawll tried to reduce the mysteries of thrift to their simple equations. In revealing these mysteries to the public he employed no subtle formulas but presented plain homilies. From his desk he announced, "Money makes money, and the money money makes makes more money . . . Save when you feel it least; have money when you need it most . . . To ask a question may make you the fool of a moment, but not to ask it may make you the fool of a lifetime."

The name of the club itself led many to enroll because it suggested that others were going to do so. Many members would not have continued saving if they had not signed up to put something away regularly each week for fifty weeks. One out of fourteen Americans today holds a coupon-savings book with the holly-bedecked emblem of the Christmas Club, and everyone who works for the parent organization belongs to a club just as Rawll did. "After all," one of them said, "Rawll taught us that nothing is pleasanter than working for Christmas."

Today, more Americans are joining Christmas Clubs in their communities than ever before. In 1949 alone there was a growth in membership of 500,000. They do not join Christmas Clubs as they do other conventional clubs. They have no officers. They have nothing to say about who joins the club. There are no age restrictions. Men, women and children of all ages have as much right to join a Christmas Club as an octogenarian millionaire or a wealthy dowager. The only requirement for a person to belong to one of these clubs is to pay "dues," and even then he decides how much he shall pay every week for his privilege of belonging to a club. The approach of each Christmas sees over 10,000,000 members calling upon 6,000-odd banks and savings institutions to withdraw their "dues." More than one billion dolars was distributed to Christmas Club members last year.

Chapter Four

Father of First Aid

Just as the whines of the Jermyn Colliery whistle echoed across the Lackawanna dale in Pennsylvania's hard coal country, an excited man with coal dust in the crow's feet of his eyes knocked on the door of a framehouse on Main Street and said to the short, auburn-haired man who answered: "Doc Shields, come quick! Someone's hurt at the mines."

A bespectacled, well-dressed man, with moustache and Van Dyck beard, Dr. Matthew J. Shields grabbed a black satchel bag and hurried out into the street. He passed other people who were headed toward the coal shaft and hurried on the swing bridge across the river. By the time he got to the shaft he had to push through a crowd of women and children. He witnessed, as he did numerous times since he left Bellevue Medical College in 1888, the strained faces, the mute suffering, the long and terrible vigil of women and children until the injured man was brought to the surface. The man, one of his legs askew, was carried out on a blackened board.

The general practitioner bent over and examined his body, cutting away the bloody rags on the injured limb. Underneath the rags and plugged into the flesh where the leg bone stuck out were wads of chewing tobacco. Splints were unknown. The doctor drew himself up. "Who did this?" he gasped. There was grim silence except for faint sobbing in the background.

Nothing in the formative years of the Jermyn doctor shocked him as much as the way the coal miners treated injuries. Why didn't the men below use a tourniquet instead of cuts of tobacco to stop the flow of blood? Why didn't they use a pick handle or a stick as a splint to prevent the broken bones from causing more damage? Why did every mine accident have to terrify the entire village? The more questions he asked himself, the more he realized that he had to do something about deaths and injuries in the mines. Why not show the miners what to do until a doctor came? From then on Dr. Shields resolved to spend his life in servitude to first aid.

Millions of persons in the United States have been saved from death and permanent injury by the crusade he launched in Jermyn,

Pennsylvania. For many years to come millions more who will never hear the name of Matthew J. Shields will be saved from death due to the first aid training he championed in the American Red Cross and the part he played in having mine rescue cars erected by the U. S. Bureau of Mines.

At first the coal miners, whom he felt needed first aid training more than any other group of industrial workers, were indifferent to his offers to train them. They thought that mine accidents were the will of God. "I'll go when my time comes," was the stock reply. But Shields knew, because he was the embodiment of self-sacrifice and healing skill, that there are many important ways of safeguarding human life just as there are ways of preventing disease.

If the miners wouldn't listen, maybe management would. Dr. Shields offered his plan to one of the foremen at Jermyn Colliery, provided the company which operated the mine, the Delaware and Hudson, would supply the bandages, splints and other materials. But the foremen said, "Your plan will cost too much."

"I assume the miners won't care about the cost as long as they don't have to leave their blood on the coal they dig," Shields answered. But the foreman continued: "How long do you suppose the company would stand for it when they hear that we're messing around with splints and bandages instead of producing coal. The miners, not the company, are to blame when they get hurt. They're careless. They don't care whether they live or not."

"But I do," interrupted Dr. Shields. "If one careless act started a fire in your mine, you'd spend thousands of dollars to drown the shaft in order to extinguish it. But you do not want to spend a few dollars to protect men's lives. What kind of Christian are you? Good day."

Dr. Shields walked away from the colliery. The furrow of determination that had separated his steady blue eyes seemed gone. A few old-timers remembered him as a disappointed crusader, slouching by his horse and buggy or walking listlessly down to the First Baptist Church with his wife Alice, a former school teacher from nearby Carbondale. But as hope slowly ebbed away, a miner who was familiar with the St. John's Ambulance Society in England stopped him on the street to talk about impromptu work, as first aid was then called. During the conversation the doctor learned that the Keg Fund, organized by several miners to pay benefits to injured members, was just the kind of group that would welcome his instruction in first aid work. Out of this body he mustered twenty-five mine workers on October 25, 1899, to start one of the most humanitarian movements in the world.

In a drab frame building, whose dusty windows bore the proprietor's name in proud letters, the members met each week. Around the floor sat 25 miners, some straight from the mines, the coal dust still runneled into their sweat-sticky faces. Shields always spoke precisely and to the point. He showed them not only how to bandage broken arms and legs, but also he demonstrated the bone structure of a human being by rattling an old skeleton. When he slashed open a fresh beef heart to show heart action, one of the miners, a short, wiry Welshman named Tom Williams, fainted. He couldn't stand the sight of blood. Dr. Shields tended to him. After that the little miner acted as a patient, sometimes stripping off his clothes, and the other men stood around as Dr. Shields demonstrated how to apply bandages.

In Shields' old stamping ground you hear countless other stories of his driving energy. You hear how, in home after home, he brought many future citizens of Jermyn into the world. William Tennis, who at 27 was the president of the initial first aid class, recalled when he met a miner's wife on his way home from work. "I hear," she said, "you were organizin' with Dr. Shields to be doctors?"

"No," Tennis replied, "we're just learning how to relieve a man when he is hurt."

"Don't you touch my husband," she warned. "I'll pelt the life out of ya the next time ya pass our coal shed."

In the early days the doctor's ingenuity saved many a patient. Dr. Shields was the lone physician upon whose skill and courage the inhabitants of Jermyn and neighboring mine patches depended. One instance involved a miner who had his right arm crushed like a boxing glove. In a makeshift operating room, with only the light of miners' lamps, Jim O'Dowd, a young member of the first class, administered ether out of a cotton-filled newspaper cone and Dr. Shields went to work with scapel and saw. Before gangrene could set in, the doctor amputated the arm and saved the miner's life.

Sometimes he had to go out on a case several miles into an almost primitive wildersnes and rush back in his horse and buggy to hold his first aid classes. To him first aid was too big ever to let go. Tirelessly he demonstrated how to treat injuries with whatever materials were at hand, and pretty soon the first aid squad of the Jermyn mine was a source of comment up and down Lackawanna Valley.

Neither Dr. Shields nor his students stopped there. On paydays they collected money at the colliery with which to buy unbleached muslin and other supplies, and out of the muslin their women made bandages for them to carry into the mines. They made first aid boxes and placed them in various sections of the mines. They persuaded the mine officials to install an ambulance station for the treatment of accidents and also to use a telephone instead of a siren to call the ambulance driver. No longer did the womenfolk crowd the mine portals to learn whose man was injured or killed.

Having set an example, the dimunitive but debonair doctor decided to spread first aid training to other mines. As he rode his horse and buggy far up in the mountains and hollows seeking converts, he posted signs on tall, black breakers of the time and place of the next class. And apt as not miners came. One of them acted as a patient and the other men stood around as Dr. Shields went through hypothetical cases. He also passed out first aid books which he wrote in collaboration with a local newspaper editor, and the miners presumably studied them between classes.

Then, just as he began to number his first aiders in the thousands, his modest home and office in Jermyn was enveloped in a fire. The water mains were frozen. Firemen were helpless. His property as well as others in the business section were burned to the ground. The miners were too poor to help him get back on his feet. Taking his wife and four children he moved twelve miles down the river to Scranton and started all over again.

Beginning from scratch was nothing new to him. He was born in Crawfordville, Georgia, on November 2, 1862, the youngest of four children of Irish parents. His father died when he was eighteen, and Matt and his mother left there to live with his elder brother in Carbondale, Pennsylvania, where sickness and disaster were never far from the coal shafts. His brother, who was a doctor of prominence, gave him a job at once, helping to give anesthetics for surgical operations or bandaging a wound. After seeing the cases brought in from the mines, Matt decided to take up medicine. He helped his brother and worked in the Carbondale railroad yards during the summers to put himself through Bellevue Medical College, not yet taken over by New York University. Then he hung out his shingle in Jermyn, halfway between Carbondale and Scranton.

After the big fire, he resumed private practice in Scranton and lectured on first aid in the evenings. Cracking the indifference of the other mining companies was not as easy as the Delaware and Hudson. "Our greenhorns won't understand you," mine foremen told him. But Dr. Shields didn't care. He knew that he had to deal largely with illiterate European immigrants, but he also knew that anyone could apply a tourniquet if he saw it done. Illiteracy didn't matter.

He badgered mining officials and carried on a continuous correspondence with various organizations to have them take up first aid training. One of the persons who thought he had a good idea was Captain William A. May, a beetle-browed civil engineer who in 1901 took charge of the Pennsylvania Coal Company, which employed over 14,000 men in 24 mines around Scranton. Dr. Shields joined the company in order to create a network of first aid teams to give prompt attention to those injured in the mines.

As he moved from colliery to colliery, Shields dreamed up a gigantic project to promote first aid. It could be made into an event of national significance. In October, 1906, two years after his removal to Scranton, he called upon each of the 36 mines operated by the Pennsylvania Coal Company and its subsidiary to hold preliminary contests in their own centers.

To him a first aid meet had all the appeal of a hog calling contest. Much good would come out of it. The race of the teams to dress the imaginary wounds of their patient would infuse the blood of athletes into the hard-working delvers of the deep. Indifferent workers would be inspired to learn more about first aid methods. The appointment of prominent mining officials and doctors as judges would give the team members a lift in the eyes of the community.

Finally eight prize teams showed up on Saturday morning, November 24, in Scranton's 13th Regiment Armory for the first competitive meet of its kind in the world. They were given different colors to wear. Their first problem involved a man insensible from gas, totally helpless, who, after being carried to good air, was to be given artificial respiration.

Almost at once, people saw from the problems given the teams how lives could be saved merely by proper handling of fractures, sprains and dislocations and artificial respiration. First by the hundreds, then by the thousands, the great and humble from near and far flocked to Scranton for Dr. Shields' marvelous first aid contests.

He did so well that he had to transfer the contests to an outdoor park to accommodate the crowds. One of the greatest joys of his life came when he persuaded Secretary of War Luke Wright to send three Army medical officers to serve as judges of the third annual meet. One of them, Major Charles Lynch, a slender surgeon of medium build, was so enthusiastic about it that he wrote a spirited report of the first aid movement in the anthracite region and outlined its possibilities in the Army hospital corps.

Soon afterwards he met the sparkplug of the American Red Cross, Miss Mabel T. Boardman, who in four years had established 35 chapters from coast-to-coast, and raved to her about the first aid movement. The same spark that ignited Dr. Shields and Major Lynch struck fire in Miss Boardman. Convinced that first aid was the key to the work of Red Cross chapters, Miss Boardman embraced the idea and asked Congress for help.

After Lynch was assigned to the Red Cross, the entire country was shocked by the terrible loss of life and limb in the mines. Four major disasters within two years took the lives of 1,013 men. Miss Boardman felt the need of pushing the first aid program so that the Red Cross could help in the event of another disastrous explosion. She tried to contact Dr. Shields, but he was busy arranging another first aid contest. So she went to Scranton to see him. She asked him if he would like to conduct first aid classes in Red Cross chapters. He needed no more encouragement.

Right away the tourniquet teacher found himself up to his neck in work. Wearing a white linen duster and a straw hat, he covered most of the major railroad centers of the country. He had railroad cars specially built to serve as traveling homes and transport his first aid equipment. He slogged through the mud with his gear, and he often was caught in a flood area where his help was badly needed. Through it all, he created a nucleus of first aid instructors.

When he returned to Washington, he found other tasks waiting for him. Dr. Joseph A. Holmes, who took over the new U. S. Bureau of Mines in July, 1910, did not have the personnel to teach first aid to men in mines, quarries, and oil fields, and badgered the Red Cross for Dr. Shields' services. Dr. Holmes, who had seen his handicraft in the hard coal fields of Pennsylvania, had implicit faith in Shields' ability to devise methods of training for mine rescue and first aid crews.

At first the Bureau of Mines did not have equipment for mine rescue work. Drs. Shields and Holmes then began their campaign to have special railroad cars built for rescue work, and ultimately six were used as bases of operations in different fields where a large number of mines were scattered over a wide area. They were equipped for carrying oxygen-breathing apparatus, making gas tests and demonstrating to students the various phases of rescue and first aid work. Dr. Shields took one car through West Virginia and Kentucky where he gave instructions, Dr. W. S. Rountree another in Alabama, Dr. A. F. Knoefel another in Indiana, and Dr. G. H. Halberstadt another in Pennsylvania.

The early clinics held in isolated coal camps were almost a one-man business. Dr. Shields did not have instructors to help, nor did he know mine foremen on his itinerary. That meant he had to go days in advance to have everything arranged, as well as select a group of key men to make up the first classes.

The classes were usually held in the mine rescue cars or schoolhouses, but sometimes, particularly in Southern communities where Negroes and whites were not allowed together in public conveyances and fraternity halls, Dr. Shields held classes for mixed groups in the woods. Although Southern-born, he placed first aid above the color line. In his course, he explained first of all the benefits of first aid, anatomy of the human body, types of shock, artificial respiration, bandages and compresses, control of bleeding. He arranged the course in such a way that in five sessions the class received enough practice dressing wounds, applying artificial respiration and other types of cases encountered in the mines. Finally he gave the class, usually not more than 25 persons, problems that it had to work out as a team.

Picking out men who were capable of absorbing and passing along to others what they had learned was not always easy. When he found men who wouldn't attend classes, Dr. Shields would hold an impromptu contest and invite widows and orphans to show the reluctant students what happened when disaster struck underground. The miners soon changed their minds about taking instructions. To arouse further interest Dr. Shields conducted a national first-aid contest, the first being held in Pittsburgh, Pa., in October, 1911. Twenty first-aid teams and four mine rescue teams from 10 states took part.

For many years doctors bore the brunt of first-aid training in the coal industry and the men who completed the course satisfactorily were awarded a first aid certificate. Neither Dr. Shields nor his associates accepted more than the minimum in salaries. The Old Boy, as his fellow doctors called him, guarded every cent entrusted to him. "If his accounts were ever checked," said one associate, "you would find where he spent every cent." But he drew other things from his work—strength at seeing his project develop, faith that first aid had saved countless lives.

Since those early years, the Bureau of Mines has trained enough key men to serve as instructors to other workers. Today there is not a place in the territory of Federal mine inspectors without an employee adequately trained in first aid. According to the Bureau of Mines, at least 200 lives of injured mine workers are saved annually by first aid crews. Had the fatality rate of the 1906-10 period continued up to the present time, however, the number of men killed in the coal mines would have been about 50,000 greater than it was.

Yet what Dr. Shields drew in strength and faith was small in comparison with what he poured into his work. From 1910 until 1931, except for two years in the Army Medical Corps during the first World War, he visited every state in the union, instructing men and women and children in the principles of first aid. He worked as hard for the Red Cross as he did for the U. S. Bureau of Mines and his work covered more ground than that of any circuit preacher. "He was the best first aid teacher we ever had," a former high Red Cross official remarked recently. There was scarcely a city he did not visit.

No doctor enjoyed his work as much as he did. He talked easily and quietly in front of classes and never used notes. He had a fine faculty for making first aid simple, and his fund of stories was suited to the bent of the class. As he rode from one section of the country to another, he never took it easy until he spoke on first aid wherever he could. In the latter part of 1915, for example, he visited 59 towns in Oregon giving instructions to employes of 82 different logging camps, in some places two groups a day, and finally moved onto the campus of the University of Oregon at Eugene. He enlisted the faculty and students in a course that taught them how to prevent an accident from happening.

In time not only coal miners and lumberjacks were taking his course, but also railroad workers and telephone men, schools and civic groups, police and firemen, farmers and homemakers. To carry on the work after he was gone, he wrote, in collaboration with others, a handbook outlining the standard methods of first aid instruction. It was published in English, Italian, Polish and Slovak. The Bureau of Mines also published pamphlets offering a modification of Dr. Shields' procedure of conducting first-aid and mine rescue contests.

The father of first aid devoted the best part of his life to the American Red Cross, and in his lifetime the Red Cross awarded 2,000,000 first aid certificates. His home most of the time was in a railroad sleeper. He had passes on all the railroads in the country and knew the train stops as well as any conductor on the road. Although he was fond of colored neckties, striped shirts, high celluloid collars and dark suits, he wasn't embarrassed if someone saw him in his shirtsleeves, a Bible showing out of

79

his hip pocket, on a Red Cross car or at a first aid contest. When he went to sleep, his friends say he snored louder than the clickety-clack of the train wheels.

The Southern-born taskmaster took turns relieving other doctors in charge of Red Cross first aid cars, two or three east and just as many west of the Mississippi. When at last the time came for him to leave, Dr. Shields took a few drinks and then nobody could reason with him. His family saw very little of him.

Once a young interne landed in Strouds-burg, Pennsylvania, with no thought other than of relieving Dr. Shields. Joe, the colored cook, carried Dr. Shields' grips to the railroad station. When the train stopped, however, Dr. Shields, still muttering in his cups, refused to get on. The cook tried to lift him up, but the doctor braced himself. The train left without him.

He continued to ride the Red Cross cars until his health started to give out in 1931. He went back to Scranton to spend the remaining eight years of his life, but he lived to see his students open roadside first aid stations for victims of automobile accidents. When he first entered the Red Cross service automobiles were not dangerous except to cause horses to run away. Today the Red Cross has approximately 2,000 first aid stations along the nation's highways and 10,500 mobile first aid units in operation, and it has 16,000 instructors specially trained in the accident prevention phase of the first aid program.

Four years after his death, more than 5,000 persons crowded on the lawn of the Jermyn Community House to witness the unveiling of the monument in honor of "the founders of first aid in America." Outside the town there is a historical marker along the highway to inform everybody entering Jermyn that this mining village of 3,519 people was where Dr. Shields started his first aid movement.

Chapter Five

Father of Basketball

Late one December morning in 1891, James A. Naismith, a 30-year-old gym instructor who awaited a class of eighteen young men, bounced a soccer ball on the gym floor of the Y.M.C.A. Training School, now Springfield College, in Massachusetts. He trained his mild blue eyes as if he were about to throw the ball into one of the half bushel baskets nailed to the over-hanging track at each end of the floor. Suddenly he heard the voice of one of his students.

"Huh!" the student grunted. "Another new game!"

Naismith's nostrils almost flared over his matted black mustache, and his hands seemed congealed on the soccer ball. "Not entirely," he finally gulped, "it's the same as trying to hit a small target with a stone. Only here you'll use a round ball."

After mustering the candidates for Y.M.C.A. secretaryships, the tall, Canadian-born instructor explained the rules of his new game. Out on the small floor, throwing the ball around with the idea of giving it to the man in the best position to pop it into the basket for a score, were two teams, each with nine men. Naismith watched as the rangy forwards dribbled under the basket, lifted their feet enthusiastically, and thrust the ball straight down into the basket. The ball smacked the bottom of the basket and spun into the balcony, with the result that the game had to be held up until someone went up there to get the ball.

"Jim," said Amos Alonzo Stagg, who was also an instructor there and later became a famous football coach, "it would be better to use peach baskets because the ball would stick in them."

Naismith got two peach baskets from the Yankee janitor and replaced the half bushel baskets. Then he called on his old classmate, Stagg, to take one of the player's positions to see how he liked it. Naismith, who served as referee and scorekeeper, tossed the ball up in the air between the two opposing centers and watched the progress. Stagg played the game as he did football. When a player shouldered him, he knocked him down.

Naismith blew the whistle and screamed, "No, no, Lonny — you got it wrong — the idea is no violence, no contact — all speed, skill and evasion!"

"You're a fine one to tell me that after the way you play football," Stagg replied.

"Now that you bring that up," Naismith said, "why did you make me play center on the football team?"

"Because, Jim, you're the one man around here who can do the meanest things with the nicest smile on your face."

Some of the gym students wanted to call the new game "Naismith ball," but the instructor nixed the idea. So, after seeing the baskets and the round ball, they christened Naismith's creation "basketball." Others called it a "sissy game," but it took all-around athletes so swift, so deft, so sportsmanlike, so richly endowed with the gift of timing and accuracy to play the grueling game that today it is the most popular sport so far as attendance goes in the country. It attracts 100,000,000 spectators each year to arenas, college and school gyms, church auditoriums and vacant warehouses. No high school is without a basketball team, and at least two universities, DePaul and Loyola, depend on its stalwart dribblers, kangaroo leapers and pivot shot artists to keep their names in the news.

How the game became so popular in many parts of the world is a tribute to the man who invented it. At first it was a peculiar situation. For a year he was an instructor in boxing, wrestling, swimming and canoeing, but despite those extracurricular activities the school for Y.M.C.A. secretaries and physical directors had nothing to interest students after the football season. They were sick and tired of twirling Indian clubs, lifting weights, and jumping horses and parallel bars. Then, because at a faculty meeting Naismith said "we can invent a new game that will meet our needs," the athletic director dropped the secretaries class into his lap. Naismith tried to interest the class in modifications of football and soccer, but the experiments left him more disheartened than when he began.

"In a day or two I would have to report to the faculty the success or failure of my attempts," he wrote. "How I hated the thought. It was worse than losing a game. All the stubbornness of my Scotch ancestry was aroused;

all my pride of achievement urged me on; I would not go back and admit that I had failed.

"With weary footsteps I mounted the flight of narrow stairs that led to my office directly over the locker room. I slumped down in my chair, my head in my hands and my elbows on the desk. Below me, I would hear the boys in the locker room having a good time; they were giving expression to the very spirit that I had tried so hard to evoke."

The noise swept away his discouragement. In his mind he reviewed the games that he had tried. Why did he fail? He observed that all team games used a ball of some kind, so he decided to convert a ball, a round soccer ball, to indoor use. But how to eliminate the roughness of handling it? Half to himself he said, "If we can't run with the ball, we don't have to tackle; and if we don't have to tackle, the roughness will be eliminated." The rest was easy. He began to foresee what the players in possession of the ball would do with it and the movements of other players. One thing came after another until he had thirteen rules for playing the game.

Little did he realize the interest the players would take in the game until Frank Mahan, one of his students who also played on "Stagg's

Stubby Christians," approached him one day before class. "You remember the rules that were put on the bulletin board?"

"Yes, I do," answered Naismith.

"They disappeared."

"I know it."

"Well, I took them," Mahan said. "I knew that this game would be a success, and I took them as a souvenir, but I think now that you should have them."

Least of all did Naismith dream that women would take up the game as they did. Some women teachers of the Buckingham Grade School entered the gallery of the Y.M.C.A. gym from the street to watch Naismith's students, some with handlebar mustaches and others with full facial adornments, scuffle around the floor with the round ball. It was only a few minutes until they were clapping and cheering for one side or the other. The next time they came to the gym one of the girls replaced her slippers with tennis shoes and marched upon the floor. She picked up a ball and lifted it toward the basket from a tricky angle. The other girls with long trailing dresses and bustles followed her and began throwing the ball around like kids in a snowball fight. Sometimes as a girl would hold the ball up and aim it at the basket, someone would reach out from behind and take the ball out of her hands. She'd look around with a surprised expression and jabbed, "Who did that?"

Witnessing this confusion, Naismith called the girls together and divided them into two sides. He started them off, but the girls didn't observe the rules. A girl frequently got the ball and ran half way across the floor to shoot at the basket. "My, my! Such a hard way to learn a game," the instructor drawled. When he thrust forward his shaggy head the cherubic angles of his face were cut in silhouette against the background.

A girl whom the others called Maude stepped up to ask the technical expert a question. Not once, but many times. She stepped up once too often, for the tall, handsome man took her hand and made her his wife on June 20, 1894. Although the former Maude Sherman continued her interest in the game, none of the Naismith's five children became basketball addicts.

College girls, however, weren't as carefree of the rules as the Springfield school teachers. The girls at Smith College, for instance, studied Naismith's first book of rules as conscientiously as their biology lessons. In it Naismith had a

picture of a playing court cut into three sections by dotted lines, and when he went to see
the girls play, he asked one of the coaches,
"Why do your girls stay in those limited
areas?"

"It's according to your diagram," said the
coach, showing him the rule book with the
dotted lines.

"Those lines?" Naismith laughed. Then he
checked himself and declared soberly, "That's
right for the women's game, not for the men,"
and the division-of-the-field rules were added to
the book. He realized that such rules would
make the game less strenuous for the amazons.

With the growth in participants, letters
poured into Naismith's office asking for help.
Most of the letters were from graduates of the
Training School who took the game with them,
first to their hometowns and then to their
respective fields of work, and they wanted to
settle a dispute about the rules. Naismith spent
a lot of time studying, developing, and clarify-
ing the rules of basketball for passers all over
the world. For the first two years the changes
in rules fell entirely on his shoulders, and the
school printed vest pocket rulebooks. In 1895,
when he left Springfield for another post, Dr.
Luther Gulick, head of the physical education

department, took over the responsibility of editing the rules. But basketball grew so rapidly that pretty soon a committee of outstanding coaches was formed to stabilize the game. It now requires a whole book to enumerate the rules of the game, and coaches have become more proficient in mastering "man to man" defense and the "zone" system.

Finding the rules in more than 30 different languages is not too hard to understand. "They're daffy about the game around the world," reported Commander William R. (Killer) Kane, operations officer of the aircraft carrier *Tarawa* when she came back from a world cruise not so long ago. "At Hong Kong we played several Chinese teams on the hangar deck of the *Tarawa*, and we picked up a couple more games at Singapore. But we got the surprise of our lives at Istanbul, the Indiana of the Middle East. The Navy played a half dozen or so games with the Turks and they licked us."

Naismith's impulse to start a new game went back to his origin in Almonte, Ontario, Canada, where he was born on November 6, 1861. At the age of eight, when he was left an orphan, he went to live with his maternal grandmother. The boys he played with used foul language, and he decided to get away from them by quitting high school and going to work. But he didn't get away from idle curses. Then he decided to enter the ministry in order to do what he could to straighten out the morals and manners of young men. He studied hard to complete three years of high school work in two and then entered McGill University in Montreal.

Some of his classmates eyed his theological ambitions with interest, and were careful not to say anything wrong when he was present. Early one morning, practicing football in extremely cold weather, the player next to him started swearing. Suddenly he stopped and turned to the football center. "I didn't notice you were there, Jim."

"I hadn't paid any attention to the swearing itself," Naismith recalled years later, "for I had heard much more competent and fluent swearing than that in Canada's lumber camps; but this realization of the discomfort of playing outdoors in cold weather changed the whole course of my life."

When he discussed his problem the Y.M.C.A. secretary at Montreal urged him to go to the Springfield training school for physical instructors. After receiving his A. B. from McGill in

1887 and completing study for the ministry at Presbyterian College three years later, he went to Springfield to devote his efforts to build clean men through instruction in athletics.

The fundamental rules he laid down for playing basketball in 1891 have changed very little since then. Other changes came within his ken, too. He himself cut the bottom out of the peach baskets because it took too long to retrieve the ball after a goal was made. The baskets were so fragile that manufacturers produced an iron hoop with leather cords, and now tennis netting is used instead of leather. The hoop was also moved six inches from the backboard, and the number of men on each side has changed from nine to seven to five.

After leaving Springfield, Naismith became physical director of the Y.M.C.A. in Denver, Colorado, where he also introduced the game of basketball. On the side he studied medicine at Gross Medical College (later merged with the University of Colorado) and was graduated M. D. in 1898. In that year he moved to Lawrence, Kansas, to become physical director and chapel director at the University of Kansas. During all this time he taught basketball to as many groups as he could reach.

Much of his subsequent progress resulted

from a conclusion he reached in the early years of basketball. "It is a game easy to play at," he said, "yet difficult to play perfectly." He not only introduced basketball on an intercollegiate basis, but he also promoted conference play throughout the Middle West. The game of basketball fascinated him the way photography, model railroading or chess fascinated other men. Though he had an M. D. after his name, he never hung up a shingle, and though he was an ordained Presbyterian minister, he never held a regular pastorate. He rolled these two professions into his teaching career.

The nearest he ever got to preaching was with the 20th Kansas Regiment on the Mexican border in 1916 and with the Y.M.C.A. service in France for two years after that. "And the preaching was rather indirect at that," he wrote afterwards. "For example, we found that too many of the boys from our camp were going into a nearby town and getting into all kinds of devilment. We set up a boxing ring near the camp entrance, and would start a lively match about the time the boys began going on leave. They stopped to watch, then begged for a chance to participate, and the next thing they knew it was time to be back in quarters. Prize fights may sound like strange preaching, but they did the work."

To Naismith basketball meant not only physical development but also moral training. Curious to know how hard the game was on youngsters, he applied his professional and investigating mind to a study of boys who came to Lawrence to play in the 1930 Kansas State High School Tournament. After the fourth championship game, his tests showed that members of the Wichita High School team, the winner of the state tournament, were in better physical condition than at any time during the tournament. Only one man was below par.

Afterwards he examined the hearts of young men who had never before played basketball. For 18 weeks, he put them through the same calisthenics and team play that a regular basketball squad would receive. Daily X-rays of their hearts, both before and after play, revealed no increase in size. Indeed, in some cases, there were decreases in heart size.

During these years, Dr. Naismith conducted another interesting investigation of a different nature and made some deductions which surprised people who went to basketball games. This time he used as his clinical material four high school teams which had been in a league tournament. His aim was to ascertain the actual number of minutes that the average high school player was in motion during a basketball game. A separate watch was kept on each of the 20 players who took part. Whenever a player stopped, his clock watcher stopped, and resumed again when the player left the bench to play. Dr. Naismith then said that basketball is more strenuous to the spectators than to the players.

The genial robust inventor blossomed into a clinic investigator who derived as much joy from meeting and working with coaches as a gallery fan derives from booing them. At a meeting of the National Association of Basketball Coaches, Naismith, honorary chairman of the National Basketball Rules Committee, asked some coaches what gave them the greater thrill: when the ball was two feet above the basket or when the ball swished through the net. Most of them said, "When the ball goes through the basket."

"You are wrong," chided Dr. Naismith. "Your highest pitch of expectancy or interest was when the ball was just above the cylinder of the basket and you wondered, "Will it go through or not?"

Although the indoor game spread quickly the world over, it took many years before bas-

ketball was played between nations in the
Olympics. The game was introduced for the
first time during the 1936 Olympics in Berlin,
Germany. In order to send the father of the
game to the German capital, the National Association of Basketball Coaches held a Naismith
Week to raise a fund for Naismith's trip
abroad. During this week colleges which approved the idea added one cent to the price of
a basketball ticket.

Despite the efforts of basketball fans, the
American Olympics committee, headed by
Avery Brundage, apparently ignored the 73-
year-old originator of the major indoor sport.
"Naismith arrived in Germany without even
a pass to see a game," charged James Tobin,
New York basketball official who was one of
the Olympic referees. "We managed to get him
a pass for all games, but it was not through
the American Olympics committee's efforts. He
was ignored there and his name stricken from
the pass list. What's more, no ceremony was
planned for Dr. Naismith."

Nevertheless, Naismith was honored on
short notice in the German Hall of Sports. He
stood on a dais while the teams of all compet-
ing nations marched by and saluted him with
cheers ranging from Mexico's "Alabeebo" to

Japan's "Banzai."

He spent the last years of his life mostly in reminiscing about old times with coaches. One time, on a visit to his son in Sioux City, Iowa, he could not resist the opportunity to drop into the Morningside College gym to see what was going on. There was a pick-up basketball game in progress and the boys needed a referee. One of them asked Naismith to serve as referee, but another boy snapped, "Come on! That old duffer never saw a game of basketball in his life." The boy was surprised, in attending a school banquet that night, to find the main speaker was none other than the founder of the game. "Well, after all," he apologized with a red face, "I guess you were refereeing basketball games before I was born."

19150

Chapter Six

Father of Correspondence Schools

Mrs. Fanny Foster, a small woman with large burning eyes, rushed into the office of the *Colliery Engineer*, in Shenandoah, Pennsylvania, with a horsewhip in her right hand. "Tom," she shouted to her husband, "the liveryman has just whipped Joel. I took the whip off him and gave him a taste of his own medicine, but I'm through with trying to protect the children from rowdies. Take us out of this mining town."

The short, compactly built man with florid cheeks looked in surprise at his wife and Joel, the oldest of their five children, who had followed her into the office. "The family's in good hands now," he chuckled, "and, if the children are worrying you, we can send them off to school."

"You mean educate them for what lies ahead in Shenandoah?" she asked.

"With all the coal in these mountains," he replied, "the children won't have anything to

101

worry about. The *Colliery Engineer* will never run out of readers." Suddenly a shrewd look came into the eyes of this white-haired editor. He picked up some of the letters from readers on his desk. For the past few years he had printed hundreds of their questions and answers on coal mining in his weekly trade journal and wanted it to become a clearing house of practical information.

"Why not?" he asked himself. "Why not make each miner's home a school and the spare hours of the evening the time for study of text material and questions. As long as I can teach mining on paper, why can't I do it by mail?"

Today, six decades later, the International Correspondence Schools stand as a monument to one man's desire to teach by mail, yet the man who directed for twenty-five years the first mail-order university in the world is all but forgotten. College educators who once scoffed at his idea of education have completely changed their attitudes. At least 150 universities, colleges and normal schools, not to mention about 450 private correspondence schools in the United States, now offer education by mail.

Thomas J. Foster not only built his university of mail-order students, but also left unanswerable the climax of his brilliant career.

Let me try to show him as he was and let you try to fathom the enigma.

In 1888, as a result of the eye-opener in his office, Foster moved his family to Scranton, 69 miles away, and rented a two-room office in the Coal Exchange Building. He discussed with Scranton businessmen the idea of building a mail-order school in that city. They were not interested. Scranton's leaders believed that their prosperity rested solely on coal mining and the county seat business.

Foster was not discouraged, for his readers still continued to send him hundreds of questions. In 1891, he decided to leave the businessmen to their smug ideas of prosperity. With horse and buggy he drove over the rough roads to stop at every coal operator's mansion and miner's shack and to talk about a school of mines. The *Colliery Engineer*, now a monthly magazine, was formed into a stock company, and within a short time Foster had some $100,000 on the subscription books.

In October, 1891, he announced the new system of correspondence lessons in his mining journal. By the sixteenth of that month, he enrolled the first student, a young coal miner named Thomas Coates of a Scranton suburb, and others soon followed. Quickly they learned the advantages of a correspondence school over night school and other means of education. They had a chance not only to make a living while they were studying, but to put into practice what they were learning while they were working. Within a year the number of students in the Colliery Engineer School of Mines, the first of International Correspondence Schools, swelled over a thousand.

After that, Scranton, set in the center of a mining area embracing a score of smaller towns and mine patches, found a new advertising medium in International Correspondence Schools. Its inhabitants began to look upon Foster, whose deep gray eyes could drill through a person and whose voice racked as if he had a piano tuner in his throat, as probably the greatest man of vision ever to walk into Lackawanna Valley. He wore dark, natty suits, bow ties, stiff-collared shirts and highly polished shoes. One of the region's early lawyers, after seeing Foster carry his five-foot-six-inch frame with jaunty vigor into his sanctum and fill him full of new ideas, remarked, "I'd been waiting for a staid man who accepted things as he found them, and what do I meet? A rubber ball out of Utopia!"

Although few persons outside Pennsylvania

had ever heard of him before 1891, Thomas J. Foster had been a minor figure in the coal belt, on and off, since he joined the Army at the age of eighteen. His father was one of the pioneers of Pottsville, the present seat of Schuylkill County, where Tom, the first of seven children, was born on New Year's Day, 1843. After serving through the Civil War, he attended Eastman's Business College in Poughkeepsie, N. Y., and then managed a shoe store which his father had opened for him.

Four years later, when he married 16-year-old Fanny C. Millet, he embarked in the printing business as an advertising solicitor, perhaps the first of his kind in the world. He called on businessmen with advertising novelties. When one storekeeper complained of not hearing from customers with overdue accounts, Foster suggested that he send them bills and originated the idea of a return address in the upper left hand corner of envelopes. The idea caught on. Today nobody except an absent-minded person would think of mailing a letter without having his return address on the envelope. Foster, however, decided that opportunities for an advertising solicitor in the coal regions were limited, and in 1870, with his brother-in-law, he moved to Shenandoah to start its first newspaper.

It seems Mrs. Foster never found peace in that place. With her bold and fearless husband, she lived in Shenandoah through the turbulent days of the Molly Maguires, outlaws of an Irish secret society who held the mining populace in terror during the seventies. Even so, her biggest job was controlling her husband's adventurous spirit. If he was not fighting the Mollies, he was investing his money in various schemes.

Once, in the middle of the 1880's, as he was prospecting for gold in Honduras, in Central America, he fell onto an ocean beach with a dose of malaria. He lay helpless at the water's edge, with the tide rising, and regained strength from the effect of salt water to crawl to safety just in time.

Although Foster was extravagant, he was a stickler for promoting the welfare of coal miners. One day in July, 1880, he regretted very much that he could not go with three prominent mining officials to investigate the cause of sickness among the coal miners of Kehley Run Colliery. All his reporters were out and he was filled with a sense of compulsion as he knuckled down alone to meet the deadline of the *Shenandoah Herald*.

The next morning he was just putting his

issue to bed when he heard yelling across the muddy thoroughfare outside. He turned to gaze out at Main Street and saw the boy running up the steps. "Mister Foster!" the boy cried. "Father didn't come home last night."

As tactfully as he could, Foster took the boy, whose father had invited him to the Kehley Run mine the day before, to his home, where Mrs. Foster could comfort the boy, and then sounded the alarm. Thousands of persons from the town and surrounding collieries rushed to the mine entrance, and the crowd began to whisper that the mine was haunted. Miners refused to enter it.

To impress their superstitions on others, some of the miners lowered a cat in a burlap bag down an air hole and raised it out, dead. But the experiment did not convince Foster. It only proved to him that the mine held deadly gases. Heading a rescue team, he improvised a method of ventilating the 130-yard slope and entered it. He found the lives of the three mining officials snuffed out by gas.

The granite-jawed newspaper editor was saddened, but not fatalistic. Twice within seven years the coal mines had taken the lives of five leading townsmen. He believed that God had saved him for some purpose in life, and it was his purpose to dedicate his life to prevent accidents in the coal mines.

From then on, he started the steady and phenomenal climb that was to revolutionize education for the working man all over the world. He blamed the ignorance of both coal operators and miners in preventing mine accidents. Despite their denunciations, he invited them to a mining lyceum and provided a place in his establishment for anyone engaged in coal mining to come for educational lectures. From his own presses he issued cheap editions of imported books on mine gases, ventilation and mining methods. He compiled the *Mine Foremen's Pocket Book*, the first book of tables and coal mining data printed in the United States, for the use of mining officials.

His booklet sold so fast that it encouraged him to start a weekly journal, *The Mining Herald*, which later became the *Colliery Engineer*. In it, in 1882, he started a column for readers who wanted to ask questions quickly, even desperately, for they might conceivably be the means of saving their lives.

Three years later, when Pennsylvania passed the first law that required new mine foremen to stand an examination for a certificate of competency, the letters to Foster's question and answers department mounted higher and higher. By the time he moved to Scranton and sold his first course of instruction he was receiving enough mail to choke a rhinoceros. Largely from these letter writers he drew the students who wanted to study the correspondence course in coal mining.

At first Foster expected his students to attend day classes at Scranton to learn the use of surveying instruments. But the students could not spare the time nor afford the expense to attend such classes. The future looked dark. In his office, after reading many disappointing letters day after day, he swung into his idea-forming process. His eyes would close, his arms would form two V's on the rolltop desk, and his head would rest on the palms of his hands. His secretary sat a few feet away, one eye on the door to chase away intruders and the other on the braintrust of Wyoming Avenue. He finally solved the problem by illustrating and explaining the use and operation of every part of the surveying instruments, and thereafter his students got all their instruction by mail.

In doing so, he found the key that unlocked the door to his larger success. For mechanical drawing and blueprint reading were the back-bone of all the engineering trades and professions. Foster employed expert writers and illustrators to prepare courses that would make architects out of carpenters, engineers out of mechanics, accountants out of timekeepers, and executives out of clerks just as his first course made mine foremen out of miners. He worked over each course, changing little details here and there, until it was as simple as if a teacher were in the textbook. He was a pioneer in visual education. Like the School of Mines, he divided the teaching into several schools, each in charge of a principal, from accounting to textiles.

Once in possession of several basic courses, Foster went after students in all places where men work. His solicitors covered a large territory. He made them part of his educational service by helping students to choose the course best suited to their needs and ambitions.

To say the least, Foster led a fertile existence during the first years in Scranton. Ideas emanated from him as freely as perfume from a carnation. He kept a scratch pad by his bed, and whenever he got an idea during the night he rose, jotted it down, and returned to sleep. When at nine o'clock every morning he arrived in his oak-paneled office, he took a drink of French Vichy water to flush his kidneys and sat down in a hard chair to clear his desk of extraneous business. His heavy mail was tackled with pencilled notations in the margins, such as "yes," "no" or "do this," and passed on to others for reply. He saved the better part of a day for promotional work.

The Scranton schoolmaster was too absorbed in his work for parties or hobbies, but once in a while he played a game of cribbage with his two sons and three daughters. About two years after his first wife died, he met Blandina Harrington, a stylish girl of natural reserve from Philadelphia, who came in one day with one of his neighbors to play cribbage, and in 1896, when she was 33, they were married. One son was born of this union.

By that time — 1899 — Foster had, instead of two rooms, a picturesque administration building on Wyoming Avenue. He also constructed a large printing plant farther down the street. He was preparing, he explained to the directors of the $1,500,000 stock company, for a big drive to open branches all over the world.

In 1901, he took his first big step, incorporating the International Correspondence Schools to handle the educational end and the International Textbook Company the publishing end of the business. The latter became the holding company of all Foster's interests. He was ready to expand across the Atlantic when, on the school's fifteenth anniversary, he revealed it had already received $29,000,000 in tuition fees.

He sent his son, Jerry, a short, happy-go-lucky fellow, overseas to study the British apprentice system, and Jerry returned with a glowing report of the opportunities in England. Before sending any of his faculty there, T. J. Foster organized a new company, the International Educational Publishing Company, with a capital of $20,000,000, to sell courses in foreign countries. Many of his students and graduates invested their savings in the foreign company, and Foster paid dividends every quarter. Students considered him a genius.

He had by now quite a board of directors gathered about him, and a stock sales department equal to any in Wall Street. By 1915 they had built up an endless chain of companies into a $100,000,000 pyramid. The number of stockholders rose in nine years from about 600 to 8,000. T. J., as the directors called him, sold stock in small lots to practically every I. C. S. student, while retaining management control with only a small block of shares for himself. He did not spare expenses to achieve results. He inspired the stock salesmen to renewed activity by banquets, conventions, and outings at fashionable resorts.

Foster was a remarkably able educator, and as a creator he had few, if any, equals. But at the head of a business enterprise, in charge of its policies and finances, it never occurred to him that he might trust his luck and extraordinary ability too far once too often. He dealt in millions as easily as his father once dealt in shoes. He seemed to think whatever he touched would make him more successful, and he put into his holding company all the money he had saved until he owned 2,000 shares.

One morning he woke up to find that students in foreign countries were dropping their studies to take up arms. The foreign school began to go badly, and Foster fell back on the International Textbook Company, now capitalized at $8,000,000, to finance I. E. P. so that he would not lose ground after the war.

In January, 1915, despite adverse cash receipts, Foster, to maintain his splendid dividend paying record, decided to pay the regular dividend to his stockholders. Before many months had gone by he saw that he would have to curtail expenses unless he could get the money to support the schools. His quick mind sprouted an idea. It was a scheme that looked wonder-

fully easy to him. He began to float a $20,000,-
000 corporation that was to teach women to
sew and cook by mail.

But it was too late. Foster did not have
the money to meet the payroll of 1,200 persons,
nor could he raise it by sale of stocks, and he
reached a financial crisis. He needed half a
million dollars to keep going. He tried desperately to get the money from the Scranton banks.
He offered $3,500,000 in real estate and assets
for the loan. "By stopping the payment of divi-
dends and by retrenchment and economies," he
said, "we will be able to repay this loan in a
short time."

The bankers were aloof. The Scranton
Board of Trade, however, realized that the
bankruptcy of I. C. S. which had brought
Scranton world-wide fame would be a severe
blow to the city. It sent three of its leading
members to investigate the school's financial
condition. Of the trio, Ralph E. Weeks, a fairly
tall, black-haired hardware merchant with a
disarming smile, was the most ambitious. He
had come to Scranton in 1895, when he had just
completed high school in Skaneateles, New York,
to enter the hardware business as an assistant
bookkeeper. Within twenty years he held not
only the confidence but the goodwill of the city.

And when, after going over the I. C. S. financial books, he said, "It is without question one of the best earning corporations in the city," the bankers perked up their ears.

They agreed to pay the debts and put up the money to save the schools, but they demanded the right to select the majority of the incoming board of directors and $1,000,000 first mortgage on the property as security for the $500,000 loan. They also asked Foster to give up financial control of the company.

Their choice to hold the purse strings was Ralph E. Weeks, who was as conservative in his business methods as Foster was bold. He promised to take the job for six months, and in that time he abolished the stock sales department, stopped follow-up offers to prospective students with cut prices, and cut the schools adrift from many overcapitalized subsidiary companies. He also slashed the salaries of top officials, including Foster's $20,000 a year salary, and thereby deepened the struggle between two groups over control of the mail-order fount of learning.

In 1916, when Weeks planned to go back to the hardware business, the attitude of the new board of directors was to elevate him to Foster's position. The directors elected Foster to chairman of the board, but instead of accepting, as he wished years later that he had, he resigned.

In 1918, after opening new offices in Scranton, he completed a course in salesmanship for representatives of Goodyear Tire and Rubber Company and later wrote a course for the paper manufacturing industry. After that, both in Philadelphia and in Wilkes Barre, he worked out courses in personality and character development to supplement the technical education that he had started, but it gradually became apparent that the shock of losing I. C. S. had somewhat subdued his self-confidence and courage. Finally, in 1928, at the age of 85, he retired.

His enormous creative power and restless imagination showed no signs of a letdown, however. In his nineties he was a thorough optimist and a man of perpetual youth, although he read prodigiously with a magnifying glass. When the end came on October 14, 1936, in an apartment in Scranton, he left half written a book which was to show the influence of technical education on our modern society. He also left the question: if he had been given time to pay off the $500,000 and if he had regained control of the schools, could he have managed the schools successfully in the future? By unseating him as president, the board of directors created the enigma, and Foster himself, by resigning, sealed it forever.

Chapter Seven

Father of Radio Preachers

When the phone rang in the pastorate of Central Congregational Church in Brooklyn one day in 1922, Rev. Dr. S. Parkes Cadman strode briskly to pick up the receiver. An official of New York's radio station WEAF was at the other end and wanted to know whether he could visit his home to discuss putting Sunday sermons on the air.

"If you can come to breakfast at my home," said the quick-witted pastor, hitching a pair of dark suspenders over his massive shoulders, "I'll be glad to see you. Otherwise, I'm too busy."

"I can make it," the radio executive replied. Within a matter of minutes he was on Dr. Cadman's doorstep in a row of brown front buildings. He had no trouble finding it, for the way to Dr. Cadman's home was well known to church leaders and other persons who came in need of advice.

"I fully appreciate what you want to do," Dr. Cadman told the visitor. "But I do not

119

think that it would be fitting for me to broadcast from the church during the hours of regular service."

"But think of the shut-ins you could reach on the radio," the other man said. "You could also reach many persons who do not attend church and bring them to the fold."

"I cannot see my way clear to do it," the pastor replied obdurately. "But," he continued, "how about the Bedford YMCA Sunday afternoon services for men?"

Dr. Cadman approached the microphone that WEAF thrust in front of him the following Sunday as a stranger. He talked in the same manner as he did from his own church pulpit, but soon people in the visible audience complained that they could not hear him when he moved out of range of the radio mouthpiece. Whereupon Halsey Hammond, the pensive-eyed secretary of the Bedford Branch of the Brooklyn YMCA, moved closer to the microphone. When Dr. Cadman moved to the right out of range of the mike, Hammond tapped him on the right leg with the toe of his shoe. When the pastor moved too far to his left, Hammond tapped him on the left leg.

To Dr. Cadman the important part of the proceedings was not the telegraphic toe but his version of the Holy Gospel. After his sermon, he spent thirty minutes answering questions which were dropped into collection baskets by members of the audience. There were business men nudging elbows with ditch diggers and students edging sidewise in their seats to peer over the burly shoulders of truck drivers and longshoremen in front of them. With his voice always under superb dramatic control, Dr. Cadman moved that mass of men in alternate tides of laughter and solemn reflection.

"What is your mental picture when you pronounce the name of God?" someone wanted to know.

"I haven't any," the minister said. "God is a Spirit. He has no form, and that which has no form cannot be visualized."

Another person asked where he could go to get a sound basis for religious faith. "To the Bible, of course," replied Dr. Cadman, picking up a copy at hand so that the questioner could see it. "Where else would a man go?" He slammed the Bible down so hard on the table that he blew every fuse in the broadcasting outfit which, in those days, was unable to handle great volumes of sound."

The physical appearance of this 55-year-old clergyman with clear blue eyes was in keeping with his resonant voice and oratorical style. His black hair, graying at the temples, was parted on the left side of his massive head, and combed largely across the crown. It was rough enough at the ends to justify the reiterated adjective, "shaggy." He was almost six feet tall, broad-browed and thoroughly impressive. He dressed well. Every one who looked into his candid eyes felt that he could confide in him.

"Have you ever thought of entering politics?"

"No," he replied to the interrogator, "that is not my business. It is not the business of any truly ordained minister of Christ."

For the hale and robust Christian leader, with all his encyclopedic knowledge of the world as a whole, and its God-seekers individually, the radio mike was just another instrument to reach more souls. Without leaving Brooklyn, where there are more churches than in any other city in the world, the radio pulpit enabled him to become the first dignitary of the church to accept radio as a new medium for religion. Yet few people know today that he was the first minister of the air.

At first Dr. Cadman used only one microphone. Then the Y.M.C.A. put up a wooden pulpit in the Bedford Branch and outfitted it with two microphones. It also put a rail around the pulpit so that the dean of religious broadcasters would not get out of bounds of the transmitter. The bar pleased him no end, for he used it as a rest between questions after the sermon was over. He answered all questions as simply as he could.

"Why," asked one questioner, "did Walter Johnson lose the last game of the World Series?"

"It is not part of God's plan," said Dr. Cadman, "that one champion shall win all the time."

As the program grew older the people at the forum asked the holy answer man questions which touched on history, biography,, literature, politics and science. The sponsors, however, tried to limit the questions to spiritual matters. Dr. Cadman was also mindful of the catholicity of his invisible audience. He changed his manner of delivery. He enunciated his words more carefully, though he still talked rapidly, and what he said was more judicial.

Nevertheless, he was expressing his views rather freely on a labor problem when a man in the audience jumped to his feet and remarked: "What do you know about such matters? You never did any hard work. You preachers have a soft snap."

"Just sit down a minute, brother," Dr.

Cadman lighted up, "and I will tell you something."

He recalled that his family was so poor that he had to enter the coal mines of Shropshire, England, as a pony driver when he was eleven. Certainly no preachers in Wellington, where he was born on December 18, 1864, were born with silver spoons in their mouths. His father and his grandfather were lay preachers, but they had to work for a living the same as other men in the surrounding lattice-and-plaster cottages.

He devoted a few hours before and after work in the coal mines to reading about religion, politics, business, military affairs, literature and world history. He read every book he got in his hands. Years later someone remarked that he had seen the statement, "I don't know," only once in Cadman's voluminous writings.

In 1885, three years after he had preached his first sermon, he laid down his pick and entered Richmond, now part of London University, to study theology. On Sundays and during vacations he and his father served neighboring chapels as lay preachers. He left England in 1890 to come to the United States. But in his future dealings with people he never lost sight of the eleven years he spent loading pony carts and swinging a pick in a mine breast.

"How," asked one of his followers, "are you able to answer all these questions so swiftly and so surely?"

"Habit, I suppose," he replied.

The candor with which he expressed himself on various subjects attracted newspaper reporters who wanted his opinions on the questions of the day. He was never reluctant to be quoted on anything. Once in connection with its offer of the complete works of Charles Dickens a Philadelphia newspaper sent a young reporter to get Dr. Cadman's opinion on the cultural and moral value of Dickens to the modern reading public. "Young man," said the Christian publicist, taking a bite out of his sandwich and shoving some letters at his secretary, "I am a stanch Dickensian if ever there was one! Take the 'Pickwick Papers.' I know of no other story that gives one that delightful, relaxed, almost uplifted feeling. A chapter of 'Pickwick Papers' is my recipe for the tail end of a trying day."

No clergyman probably worked as hard as he did to spread religion. Besides shepherding his flock of parishioners in Brooklyn and addressing the radio audience on Sunday afternoons, he headed the Federal Council of Churches in America, conducted a daily syndicated column, wrote advance copies of his sermons for the *Brooklyn Eagle*, reviewed religious books and wrote some himself, answered hundreds of letters every week, and traveled widely on lecture tours.

"He lives in a whirligig world," said Professor William J. Thompson, Drew Theological Seminary, "and rivals an acrobat who keeps four balls flying in the air, while upon an instrument of percussion he makes a joyful noise with his feet. A man with a giant's strength could do what he does. None other can."

For his vacations he usually went abroad to attend some world conference of Christian leaders. One year, though, he went with his wife and three children to their summer home in Lakeville, Connecticut. Mrs. Cadman thought he was going to spend his time relaxing and fishing.

The first morning he took his fishing rod and started out. He was gone all day. Next day the same thing. When he brought no fish home for several days, Mrs. Cadman became suspicious. She went out to see where he spent his time. With his boat moored between boles of pines, she found the thwart loaded with

books and the clergyman himself hard at work
on a manuscript.

With all the time he devoted to extra activities, Dr. Cadman was still the most approachable and human of clergymen. He was a good
listener as well as a voluble talker. But most
of all he never let his parishioners down. Scores
of them called at his home every week with
their problems. He once canceled an important
lecture engagement and returned a thousand
miles home to attend the funeral of a member
of his church. The Central Congregational
Church, one of the most important Congregational parishes in the world, was not the only
pastorage he ever had.

His first pulpit was under the peaked roof
of a deserted church in Millbrook, a small
village in Duchess County, New York. It paid
him $600 a year. To supplement his income
and bring his wife from Shropshire, he took
charge of another Methodist church at Verbank,
three miles away. Within five years he was
preaching to crowded houses at both places at
different hours on Sunday, and his salary was
twice as much as before. His fame as a creator
of pulpit epigrams slowly grew. "We have become sermon tasters," he said, for example,
"instead of Christian workers."

His next charge in Yonkers, where he helped to clean the saloon gang out of city government, was of short duration. For the trustees of Metropolitan Temple offered the Yonkers parish a $5,000 bonus to release him. Dr. Cadman came to New York City and within six years added the names of 1,600 members to the weak parishes in the downtown section. Then he went to Brooklyn.

All his life he was a crusader, and while in his latter years his zeal was expended mostly for the Christian movement and speaking on the radio, his crusading for peace cannot be overlooked. He served as chaplain to an infantry regiment on the Mexican border in 1916 and believed in military preparedness until 1926. In that year, although he was invited to appear on the commencement program of the New York Military Academy at Cornwall, he was barred after voicing his opposition to military training in the schools. So angry did the die-hard militarists become at their former brother-in-arms that one Sunday afternoon they stormed his radio forum and hissed until the police reserves ejected them.

But there were hosts of others who regarded his pacifism with genuine admiration. In 1927 he urged President Coolidge to arbitrate the nation's differences with Mexico, but the chief executive refused. From the radio pulpit the peace advocate swung into action. Telegrams and letters poured into Washington. The nation's lawmakers, feeling the impact of Dr. Cadman's invisible audience, finally passed a resolution for arbitration and thus probably averted a war with Mexico.

The following year he was signally honored when the National Broadcasting System, which then operated forty stations on a national hook-up, named him its official radio preacher. Each Sunday morning he broadcast from the NBC studio at Rockefeller Center and then raced back to his own church for the eleven o'clock service. The vast audience inspired rather than awed him, and kept him in concert pitch. He had a number of secretaries to answer the thousands of letters addressed to him every week, and he himself sat up until two or three o'clock in the morning to answer the tough ones. Thrice a week a masseur came to rub and knead the tenseness out of his body.

For more than 500 radio sermons he received no pay, yet he was the highest paid minister in the country. He received $40,000 a year from his church, and many felt that he was worth it. His talks were vital and dynamic.

He drew his examples and figures of speech both from life and books, and those who heard him received a tonic for better living. He reached a body of people stretching from the fishermen's villages of Maine to the ranchers' homesteads of Arizona and from the lumberjack's camps of the Northwest to the palmshaded homes of Florida.

Sometimes he was compared to Henry Ward Beecher, a Brooklyn clergyman of wide personal influence in the public affairs of the antislavery, Civil War, and reconstruction periods. He laughed humbly when one writer mentioned it to him. The radio posed certain problems for him that the Civil War minister did not have to face. But in comparing his method of preparing sermons and lectures with Beecher, there was a little similarity. Beecher wrote his sermons in the form of brief notes in bold and hasty handwriting, and one of his best pulpit masterpieces was prepared in about two hours. Dr. Cadman wrote his sermons more fully, but, like Beecher, he rarely used a manuscript in delivery. His purpose in writing them was to organize the material which, once written, remained fixed in his mind.

Above all, the former English coal miner was humble and grateful for the vast opportunities of carrying his message on the radio. "If one uses the radio merely to preach special doctrinal views," he commented, "he will fail. On the other hand, if he uses radio to broadcast the great basic principles of religion and of the welfare of the world, he finds in it an agency of unprecedented value."

Dr. Cadman also saw the Hitlerite menace to his creed and to the world early. For saying what he saw and felt the Nazi leader banned one of his books, *Adventure for Happiness*, in Germany. By this time the Bishop of the Air was too old to render much service to the anti-Nazi movement. His hair was no longer glossy black. It was iron-gray. His figure was no longer trim and erect. But his voice could be depended to rise and fall in crescendo.

His phenomenal memory began to fail him. When he was ten minutes late for a Lenten service in a neighboring Brooklyn church, he apologized like this: "My secretary and others have told me I was to be here at 12:30. I ought to have known better; I've been here before. But, sometimes, things escape the memory of an old man."

In July, 1936, despite recurring gall bladder trouble, he decided to attend the summer union services of the Methodist Episcopal Church in

Plattsburg, New York. After delivering a stirring address, he collapsed on the stage and was rushed to a hospital. He never regained consciousness. Many years have passed since his death, yet he is less known today than the other Brooklyn pastor who died sixty-odd years ago.

Chapter Eight

Father of the Movies

On the first Sunday in June, 1894, a fairly
tall brunette with a Grecian profile and a secre-
tarial figure decided to take her beau, who had
been taking pictures of her all afternoon in
a Washington, D. C., park, to see her married
sister. They had barely entered the home when
the gallant, red-haired suitor saw his girlfriend's
niece, Annie, blowing bubbles.

"Let me take your picture?" he asked.

The five-year-old girl looked up in surprise
at her aunt's boyfriend, C. Francis Jenkins, a
27-year-old stenographer in the Life Saving
Division of the Treasury Department, and shook
her head. He offered her a nickel, but the girl
still said no. At last he thought of the Phantoscope, as he called the motion picture projector,
he had just invented. "If you'll let me take your
picture," he finally implored, "I'll show you
living pictures of a little girl in a pretty costume dancing on the wall."

"All right," Annie said.

When he projected the first motion pictures

from flexible film in a Washington darkroom, Jenkins had no idea he was starting a billion-dollar business. Nor did his three guests. The strips of film as they passed before perpendicular rotary lenses were illuminated by an incandescent lamp and the pictures were flashed upon a silk handkerchief which served as a screen on the wall. As the lamp blinked and the Terpsichorean movements grew more erratic, the three witnesses began to giggle and laugh. "How wonderful!" Annie exclaimed at one point. "Are you going to show pictures of me blowing bubbles, Mr. Jenkins?"

Few businesses have had a more spectacular rise than the movies. Within two years of the time Jenkins took out a patent for his Phantoscope in 1894, three times as many patents were issued on motion picture projectors as were issued in the previous thirty years. Each of the 25,000 theaters in the United States has a prototype of Jenkins' Phantoscope in its projection room. The standards of motion picture projection were also laid down by Jenkins and others when he founded the Society of Motion Picture Engineers in 1915. Nothing in recent times has influenced our manners and morals, created our fads and fashions, and shaped our thoughts and emotions as much as the movies.

FATHER OF THE MOVIES

In 1949 about four billion tickets were sold to movie goers in the United States.

"The movies," said Denis W. Brogan, professor of political science at England's Cambridge University, "are innocently the most revolutionary instrument that has come from America since the Declaration of Independence."

If C. Francis Jenkins is forgotten as the father of the movies, at least no one can blame it on his lack of inventiveness. For no man contributed more to movies, both celluloid and radio, than he did. He stuck with it until his death in 1934 and to the end there were as many ideas and inventions in his mind as there had been back in the cobblestone and gaslight days when he bent his five-foot-nine-inch frame over a sputtering projector to win a tiny girl's favor.

He did not profit from them until the closing years, when age, promoters and a heart disease combined to shut him out from the world of radio movies. The rest of his career was composed of a continuous succession of new inventions. Among them were the multipassenger car, the parafined paper container, an altimeter, a braking device for airplanes and an automobile self-starter. He was one of ten men in this country who took out more than

400 patents. He was also an amateur architect, designer of machinery, a mechanical draftsman, and a registered patent attorney.

In his more than 400 patents Jenkins suffered enough setbacks to start a colony of frustrated inventors. He lost enough income from his patents to support a small town bank, and he learned to judge the value of his experiments with the appreciation of a connoisseur. There was, for example, the time he invented a ball bearing and refused to sell it for $750. While holding out for a higher price, someone invented the ball bearing in a cage and captured the sale from under Jenkins' nose.

As a result he decided to grab every bona fide offer that came his way, only to learn that it sometimes boomeranged. Once he sold a milk-bottle capper for $10,000 and a royalty of $2.00 on each capper sold. When he failed to receive royalties, he turned the contract over to a lawyer for action. The lawyer was a shyster. He surrendered the contract to the promoter and pocketed the cash. That was the last Jenkins heard of him.

The resilience of this touch-and-go inventor, who for years had recorded his work in the Patent Office as often as Thomas Edison and Nikola Tesla, began to take shape when he was born near Dayton, Ohio, in 1867. His sturdy Quaker parents moved to a farm in the wilderness outside Richmond, Indiana, when Francis was two. One day, when he was about twelve, his father took him into the fields to locate the trouble with the grain mower. The trouble was a hot bearing, and the young Jenkins belittled the farmhands who couldn't locate it, and he felt that it diverted him from his real purpose, which was to make something new.

"That is thy gift," his father said, "and to thee it is no great credit."

At the age of sixteen, when the heat was on for him to keep all the farm machinery in order, he fled Earlham College, a Quaker institution situated in Richmond, and didn't stop until he got to Oregon. A lad with a variety of talents, he had no difficulty finding work in the great logging camps of Oregon and Washington.

Footloose and with a great love of the outdoors, Charles Francis Jenkins ran a wreck train in Oregon, mined silver in the Sierra Nevadas, drove a stage coach during the soiree of Apache massacres, and punched cattle in Texas. On one of his annual visits back home, he took a civil service examination, and some months after, in Mexico, received a delayed telegram which notified him of his appointment to a clerkship in Washington, D. C.

In the nation's capital, where no one seemed to work very hard at anything, he soon became secretary to Sumner I. Kimball, walrus-mustached founder of the U. S. Life Saving Service. His office colleagues thought he was queer because he contended that he could make pictures move. Thereafter he spent all his spare time in photography.

He took pictures of Arthur J. McElhone, who worked in the Life Saving Service, and then tried to reproduce McElhone's tumbling, pole vaulting and other athletic activities from the film to a makeshift screen. He also paid two chocolate-skinned boys to turn somersaults while he photographed them. It took him four years altogether to develop the Phantoscope.

When he went down to the Patent Office on January 12, 1894, to patent it, he spent the last dollar in his pocket. He could not save enough from his meager government salary to fulfill the promise of the motion picture machine and, after his first financial backer died in 1893, his future seemed dark. He had trouble finding another angel until he was introduced to Thomas Armat, a Washington real estate dealer, and Jenkins asked him to come to his lodging place to see his Phantoscope. It had some defects, Jenkins confessed, but he could easily solve them with money to buy materials. Armat was impressed, and on March 25, 1895, signed an agreement with Jenkins to finance the invention and market it at the proper time.

For several months, working together and alone in their spare time, Jenkins and Armat hacked away at the Phantoscope to produce a projector whose every film would stand like a cameo on the wall. As it was, the projector, with an ill-covered lamp, did not show the film evenly. They rearranged one or two gears for continuous movement of film on a screen. But it still didn't work.

Next, Jenkins' idea was to use a circular disc from his original model and add a pin to crank the disc one revolution at a time, with a brief rest in between, to present the pictures with the proper illumination on the screen. But that didn't work, either.

Further experimentation took more money out of Armat's pocket. He felt that he now had more to say in the experiments, and the partnership started to rip at the seams. On temperamental grounds, Armat and Jenkins were worlds apart. Where Jenkins was hasty and temperamental, Armat was methodical and persistent. Where Jenkins was a mechanical creator with few equals, Armat was a mercenary inventor. It was inevitable that the young minds should clash. Eventually they made an eccentric cam to give the film the jerks of the intermittent movement required. When they were done they had, whatever their personal differences, a satisfactory working model. For it they applied for letters patent on August 28, 1895, and relied on a model making shop to give them three just like it.

With so much time and money in this projector, the two men decided to go to the Cotton States Exposition, in Atlanta, Georgia, because it promised large crowds for the trial of their flickers. They set up a motion-picture hall on the midway, painted it bright green, and hung up a large sign in front: "Moving Pictures Inside. Price, 25 cents." The people listened to a barker who tried to sell the wonders of living pictures, smiled incredulously at the sign, and passed in promenade. For three days nobody entered the theater.

Then the concessionary collector came around to discuss business, and when Jenkins and Armat told him that they had no proceeds, he offered them a hall in a smaller place. To convince him that they needed a large place, the movie pioneers took him into an empty theater and showed him the program again and again. The collector was convinced.

"I don't think the people outside know what moving pictures are," he said. "If you could only find some way of letting them know what they were going to see, you could fill the place."

Jenkins and Armat then realized that the only way to advertise their invention was to open the show free to all. They took down their sign and hung up another one: "Come Inside and Rest — And Look at Moving Pictures Free of Charge."

People hesitated, then walked in, and when the lights were clicked off in the theater they were sorry they had. They thought they were being robbed. Some hurried out, and others stayed when animated pictures appeared on the wall. Once they saw the pictures, a ballyhoo artist from a side show asked them to leave a quarter in the box at the exit if they enjoyed the exhibition. The first demonstration raised fifteen dollars, and thereafter more and more people came in to see the novelty.

In November, Armat, after reading in the newspapers that Jenkins had taken one of the three projectors to Indiana and exhibited it in a Richmond jewelry store, called on Jenkins at his boarding house. The rugged Hoosier, his suit unpressed and his shaggy red hair curling over his collar, pushed away from his desk.

"What are you drawing?" Armat asked.

"A new projection machine," Jenkins replied. "When I complete it I am going down to the Patent Office with it."

"Oh, no, you won't," Armat retorted. "The machine belongs to me as much as it does to you."

"But not this one," Jenkins said. "As for the contract, how can I work with you when you're not providing the money you said you would? We're already over two thousand dollars in debt."

From then on Jenkins and Armat faced each other in court instead of across the workbench. First of all, the Patent Office refused to give Jenkins a patent on his improved projector. Armat, on the other hand, negotiated a deal with Raff and Gammon, selling agents for the Edison coin-in-slot peep show Kinetoscope, to manufacture their jointly owned projector under the name of Vitascope in Edison's West Orange, N. J., plant. Through court after court the differences of the two inventors were dragged. Armat offered to buy Jenkins' interest in the joint patent for $2,500. That was as much as Jenkins owed for materials, labor and tools. He demanded $10,000. In the end, tired of law suits, injunctions and other troubles, he settled for about half this sum. Armat went on to make half a million dollars out of this invention.

Even so, Armat still was not out of his hair. When, in 1895, the Franklin Institute in Philadelphia was about to pin the Elliott Cresson gold medal on his chest for the invention of the Phantoscope, Armat put in a protest. He claimed he was the inventor of the motion picture projector instead of Jenkins. The Philadelphia organization held up the award until a sub-committee investigated. Armat submitted no papers to prove his claim. So, in 1898, Jenkins received the medal of honor. Fifteen years later, in recognition of the value of this invention, Franklin Institute also bestowed the John Scott medal upon Jenkins.

With the motion picture projector out of his hands, Jenkins still found ways to contribute his talents to filmdom. To meet the slowly increasing demand for film in the nickelodeon days, he made film perforators for two of the largest film manufacturers in the world. Jenkins was so poor when he personally delivered the first one to George Eastman, a film pioneer of Rochester, New York, that he could not buy his own breakfast. At the same time he built the best movie cameras in existence, and supplied them to Herbert Miles, the first movie cameraman to enter the Klondike; Burton Holmes, the noted world traveler and lecturer, and countless others.

During his lean years Jenkins also cranked away at a movie camera to lift the motion picture from the status of infant and unrefined flickers to that of educational, scientific and news value. He was the first to attempt photographing the flight of a projectile. He set up his camera in a bombproof shelter, but the concussion of the first discharge from the gun shattered the camera. Another time he took his photographic traps to the harsh mesas in northeastern Arizona to capture the snake dance of the Hopi Indians on film. In 1908, when the great White Fleet came home, he went down the Potomac to Hampton Roads with President Theodore Roosevelt to take news pictures of the fleet the Rough Rider sent around the world for the sake of peace.

Jenkins never brushed aside an idea. At Hampton Roads, where newspapermen were as thick as ships, a reporter asked him why he didn't design a projector for educational use. As a result of this discussion, the resourceful, optimistic inventor designed what was called the Graphoscope. This portable projector was invaluable during the first World War to entertain and instruct servicemen in cantonments and aboard troop ships. The *USS George Washington*, which carried President Woodrow Wilson to France and back after the peace conference, had three of these motion picture projectors.

After the war, Jenkins bought a surplus Curtis flying boat, the first of four planes that he owned in the next eight years, to study the use of motion picture cameras aboard airplanes. Although past fifty, he learned to fly. The discovery of the prismatic ring, a new contribution to optical science, was the direct outgrowth of Jenkins' interest in aviation.

This new shape in glass gave a stationary beam of light impinging on one side an oscillating motion on the mergent side in rotation. If it can produce light, argued Jenkins, there is no reason why it shouldn't enable him to see in one place what is happening in a distant place. And so he began to seek a technique, which, like drawing straight lines on paper over an Indian head nickel to produce the figurehead, would transmit pictures by radio.

In this quest he was different from other

inventors. His goal was to transmit images by radio, splitting it two ways — radiovision and radio movies. The first meant the transmission of images by living subjects, while radio movies meant sending pictures by radio from flat photo negative plates. Many inventors, on both sides of the Atlantic, were interested mainly in television — the transmission of living images by wires. Jenkins devoted himself to radio because wires were not readily available.

Jenkins, who sat tirelessly in his laboratory at 1519 Connecticut Avenue, in Washington, D. C., finally discovered the magic of the air waves. By telephone he transmitted the portrait of Secretary of the Navy Denby to the Navy's radio station in Anacostia where it was changed into radio signals and broadcast. In his laboratory Jenkins picked the signals out of the air with a radioviser, a little box consisting of a pair of glass discs rotating on a motor, and changed them into the original light values. When these were recorded photographically, he was ready to send pictures from city to city. On March 23, 1923, the first radio photos of President Warren G. Harding, Secretary of Commerce Herbert Hoover, and Governor Pinchot of Pennsylvania were transmitted from Washington to Philadelphia, a distance of 130 miles, and they were printed in a special five o'clock edition of the Philadelphia *Evening Bulletin.*

William Jennings Bryan, in thanking Jenkins for a copy of his radio photograph, quipped, "What is there left to be discovered?" The question teased Jenkins. For almost at once he started to figure out how to send motion pictures by radio. He imagined he could reproduce distant scenes and events on theater screens, and on smaller screens in homes, simultaneously with the event itself. He predicted that the day would come when movies could be distributed from Hollywood to every theatre of the country by radio instead of by film. He also prophesized that when his development lengthened the reach of the radio the President of the United States may look on the face of the King of England as he talks with him.

Nevertheless, the father of the movies set out to develop radio movies to be broadcast for entertainment in the home. He didn't intend to be sidetracked. Within two years he was ready to demonstrate it. A group of distinguished public figures had come to Jenkins' laboratory to witness the first demonstration of radio movies. Jenkins walked back into the receiving room to see that everything was working.

To his consternation the set was dead. There were no radio movies. What would he tell his guests? Crestfallen, he greeted the first visitor, Dr. George M. Burgess, director of the U. S. Bureau of Standards, and as he led him to the room where the receiver was located he tried to build up an excuse for the balky machine. As he opened the door his eyes popped out. The blades of a miniature Dutch windmill, installed in front of a radio in Anacostia, were seen propelling on the screen.

As Secretary of the Navy Curtis D. Wilbur watched the image of a revolving propeller miles away, long the fantastic dream of science, he turned to Jenkins and remarked, "I suppose we'll be sitting at our desks during the next war and watching the battle in progress."

"That's perfectly possible," Jenkins nodded.

He continued his experiments with the result that on July 2, 1928, he began from his laboratory and later from a five-kilowatt station in nearby Maryland, the first regular broadcast of radio movies in the nation to the few persons having picture receivers. The stars of his silhouette studio, unique in the movie art, were recruited from his laboratory staff. Every evening people waited for Jenkins' stars to come on.

This was the principal objective of his life
—to bring radio service to the eye as others
were for the ear. He was profoundly interested
in human intercourse. He believed that the
more people saw of one another the less a menace they would be to society. He thought the
radio would make persons in various parts of
the world familiar to one another.

He also thought that everyone should own
a radio-seeing set. For that reason he sold his
patents to the Jenkins Television Corporation,
originated by a New York banker, for $250,000
in cash and millions of dollars in stocks. He
was elected vice president in charge of research,
the highest paid officer in the company, but he
felt out of place in an impersonal corporation.
Two years after selling his patents he resigned.

But he could not rest. He went back to his
old laboratory and started to work on a form
of scanning disc. The long and untiring work
overtaxed his heart and for the last three years
of his life he suffered chronic muscular spasms
of the chest. Despite angina pectoris disease, he
tried to continue experiments with a home
movie and sound recording camera.

Always he was the inventor. Once, when
he visited his mother in Indiana, she told him
to "stop messing around" and go to work. She

detested the word inventor. Years later, when his inventions brought him enough to buy a modest home in Washington, he asked her for a title to his occupation. "Well," she replied, "thee is a finder-out."

Chapter Nine

Father of the Funnies

Early Sunday morning, November 18, 1894, New Yorkers stopped to gape at the colored newspapers for sale on the street corners. The newsboys usually filled the air with barks of the day's headlines, but what they now shouted left the customers in a dither. Slowly a man drew two pennies out of his pocket and shoved it into the carrier's hand: "Give me the funny paper."

Before long the piles of colored newspapers were gone. The newshawks sold three times as many copies as they did on previous Sundays. With laughter in Hell's Kitchen, Washington Heights, the Bowery and other sections of Peter Stuyvesant's island, the antics of a clown and a dog on the front page of the art supplement struck the public fancy.

"Origin of a New Species," as the comic strip was called, showed the clown and the dog enjoying a hearty lunch and falling asleep under a shady tree. Then a large snake crawled down from the tree and swallowed the dog. The tug of the dog's leash in his hand awoke the clown. He cut holes in the snake's belly to get the dog's feet out, and led the dog whose body was still encased in the snake out of the woods. Maybe it all was grotesque, but the readers liked it.

The funny section that sent them stampeding for the *New York World* seemed fantastic to them; it would have seemed more so if they could have looked into the future. For as they laughed at the comic art, they were cutting out a new career for a little-known illustrator named Richard F. Outcault.

Outcault had started something that was to end up as one of the most popular forms of entertainment in the world. Every Sunday — not to count 30,000,000 daily readers of black and white comic strips—40,000,000 Americans sprawl on the floor or curl up in an easy chair to pore over the colored comic supplements in their newspapers. Only the stately *New York Times* out of all the Sunday papers does not print comic strips. The impact of comics on our lives is no easier to hold back than Niagara Falls would be with a spoon. Five persons read the funnies to every one who goes to the movies.

The core of this laugh industry grew when

Outcault's friend, Roy L. McCardell, who in 1893 had seen a colored supplement with cartoons and pictures of the World's Fair in the *Chicago Inter-Ocean*, suggested colored funnies to Morrill Goddard, brisk, young editor of the *New York World*. "I have no artist to do it," replied Goddard, "and all the good comic artists are under contract to *Life* and *Judge*."

"Comic artists come to *Puck* everyday," said McCardell, who was at the time on the editorial staff of the humor magazine. "I'll get one of them for you."

McCardell went to see Outcault at his home in Morningside Heights, where they had previously made up a full page sketch for a magazine involving the changeover from horsecars to electric streetcars, and outlined his idea. Outcault was a mild, easy-going artist who adorned his lean, five-foot-eight-inch frame with a velveteen painting jacket and a Barbizon beret. His eyes were deep gray, his hair was chestnut, and in repose his face had the look of a country minister. He was 31, seven years older than McCardell, and played in an amateur theatrical group whenever he got a chance. The pen and ink draftsman agreed to meet McCardell's challenge of comic art.

With Goddard and McCardell, he laid out

the first comic strip ever printed. Goddard was so pleased that he paid each man $100. From then until he drew a different comic strip, Outcault received $100 a week for his work. In between his comic art, he accompanied reporters, one of whom was the daring Nellie Bly of world-girdling fame, to illustrate the news of the day, such as fires, train wrecks, murder trials and accidents. With newspaper seasoning he developed speed and self-confidence.

After presenting a number of Sunday color pages, each complete in itself, he got a story called "McFadden's Flats" to illustrate. He drew a page showing the characters in a typical New York tenement district. He called it Down in Hogan's Alley, a line lifted out of a popular Irish song, and the humor it exerted upon newspaper readers stemmed from a burlesque twist that the artist was able to give to topics in the public eye. The dwellers of the alley, for example, first rehearsed the wedding of Consuelo Vanderbilt and the Duke of Marlborough.

The series was not read with regularity until one of the characters, a flop-eared, two-toothed tenement waif in an ankle-length night-shirt, attracted the eye of William J. Kelly, foreman of the *World's* color-printing plant. He complained the kid always appeared in a wishy-washy color. Charles W. Saalberg, an artist who had some of Outcault's panels in his hands, swathed the urchin's gown in solid yellow. Next Sunday, February 16, 1896, the Yellow Kid, as the comical kid was soon called, caught the public imagination on the run.

In succeeding strips Outcault spotlighted the Yellow Kid in gutersnipe antics and the comic strip attracted regular readers. It was the talk of New York. Outcault printed on his yellow gown such impudent legends as "Dey aint nuthin but features left on my face. I'm going to quit. Dey aint no system in dis game." The circulation of the *World* soared higher and higher, and well that it did. Joseph Pulitzer, the publisher, needed it in the midst of a circulation war with William Randolph Hearst, who in the fall of 1895 had entered the New York field with the purchase of the *New York Journal*.

Hearst fumed in his den on Newspaper Row. He had no feature as popular as the Yellow Kid to increase circulation and decided to spend wads of a large mining fortune to show New York what a two-fisted, high-pitched editor out of the West could do. He met his first rebuff when he tried to hire the artist of Yellow Kid. "I won't leave Goddard," Outcault said simply. Hearst then called Goddard to his suite in the Hoffman House and offered to engage him and his entire staff.

Goddard, who for ten years had been working on the *New York World*, said that he could not leave Pulitzer's financially strong newspaper for Hearst's unknown enterprise. Whereupon the tall publisher reached in his vest pocket and handed Goddard a crumpled $35,000 draft on the Wells Fargo Express Company.

"You can take all or any part of that to bring your staff to the *Journal*," he said in a high pitched voice.

Next day Outcault joined Goddard and went to work for the *Journal*. Pulitzer refused to give up the Yellow Kid, and engaged George B. Luks, afterwards a distinguished portrait painter, to continue the comic strip in his Sunday paper. The Yellow Kid then appeared in two different comic strips, and each paper tried to outdo the other. While Pulitzer's funnies were confined to four pages, Hearst installed a new color press to print an eight-page colored comic supplement that would make, as he said, "the rainbow look like a lead pipe."

Outcault brightened the pages of the art supplement with the antics of the Yellow Kid. His speeches, instead of appearing in a balloon as they do now, were lettered crudely on the yellow nightshirt. "Composin' music dese days is easy," one of them said. "All yer have ter do is ter buy Gilbert and Sullivan and de 'Chimes of Normandy' and yez kin rite an opera." Imitating a policeman, dropping ice down a girl's back, pouring flour all over a boy's new suit, acting as a mascot for Princeton and strumming a harp for the 400 were done every Sunday to make the readers laugh. But it seems Outcault often made devils out of his younger readers, for they went around imitating the Yellow Kid.

It was too much for parents and preachers who saw in the bad boys the toughness of the slums. "I cannot permit my children to see your vulgar comics," wrote an irate subscriber. Hearst did not care. The way he combined the Yellow Kid with streaming headlines and sensational stories to increase circulation was called "yellow journalism." To combat this type of journalism, the *Christian Science Monitor* was started up in Boston and kept funnies, crime and disaster news out of its pages.

After the Yellow Kid became a smash hit, Outcault moved his wife and two children to Flushing, Long Island, and did his work at home. When required to boost the Yellow Kid three times each Sunday, he almost quit the

Hearst paper. He didn't know from one week
to the next what his next comic strip would
involve. The kid of his exhuberant fancy began
to fade. Luckily for him the courts, after a
bitter legal battle between Hearst and Pulitzer,
ordered Hearst to transfer the Yellow Kid to
the *New York World*. Taking it off his hands
saved the artist from going entirely dry.

After that he mingled little in New York
life. His social life was limited exclusively to
small parties. He spent several months just
sitting around and thinking up new situations.
Finally he devised another strip, which he
named Por Li'l Mose, dealing with the frustra-
tions of a Negro kid, and it was launched in
the *New York Herald* in 1901.

This Sunday page did not go over as well
as the Yellow Kid, and the father of the Sunday
funnies began to wonder if he would have to
surrender the place to other comic strip artists
who had come up from the drafting rooms.
Fred Opper drew "Happy Hooligan;" James
Swinnerton, "Little Jimmy," and Charles W.
Kahles, "Hairbreath Harry." Pretty soon Outcault didn't have to wonder. Rudolph Dirks,
who invented a couple of bad boys known as the
Katzenjammer Kids for the *Journal*, took the
leadership away from him for a time.

Outcault, who was born at Lancaster, Ohio, on January 14, 1863, was back where he had started. At fifteen, with his art training half completed at McMicken School of Design, in Cincinnati, he took a job painting landscapes on office safes in the ateliers of Hall's Safe and Lock Company. After tiring of painting Hall's name over and over again, he switched to the *Cincinnati Enquirer*, where he did utility art work. By the summer of 1888 Outcault, whose wages were twenty-five dollars a week, was reporting and illustrating feature stories.

That year Thomas A. Edison sent some electrical inventions for display in the Cincinnati Exposition, and Outcault went out there to draw pictures of the gadgets as well as to make comments upon them. When his layout from the *Enquirer* was sent to Edison, the electrical wizard was so impressed that he telegraphed Outcault to take the next train for Menlo Park, New Jersey.

"Young man," asked Tom Edison during the interview, "what do you want to do in life?"

Young Outcault stood there a moment, his narrow, pointed face softened by friendly eyes and a heavy shock of hair, and the Menlo wizard said, "Go ahead and tell me."

"Paint art with a big A," replied Outcault.

As a result Edison sent the young artist to study in Paris, where he shared a studio with a promising English poster artist, Dudley Hardy. Within a year he had absorbed the painting spirit of the Parisian Latin Quarter. He returned home with the ensemble of a Barbizon artist.

Soon Outcault was foregoing oil painting in favor of trips to see Mary Jane Martin, his childhood sweetheart, in Lancaster. They were married in their hometown on Christmas Day, 1890. His prospects hardly justified his action and he immediately set out with his bride to better them in New York. He landed a job drawing-to-scale working parts of dynamos for the *Electrical World*. He drew comic pictures at night and submitted them to such humor magazines as *Truth* and *Puck*. Three years later, in an economy wave, the *Electrical World* notified him that it was closing the art department for the summer months.

He turned to free-lance work. One day, when he was in the offices of *Truth* with a comical sketch, he met Roy McCardell, then also free lancing. On their rounds of editorial markets, they got a tip that a magazine was preparing a special issue to show the advantages of new electric cars over horsecars. They decided to do a full page on speculation. Outcault drew a cartoon of new trolley cars passing through city streets and country lanes and an old-fashioned horsecar on the scrap heap. McCardell wrote the poetry.

When they took the layout down to the offices of the *Street Railway Journal,* the editor liked the cartoon and the verse except the last line, "And the wheels are clinking loudly at the joints in the tracks." He thought it might offend advertisers. Outcault engaged the editor in a conversation while McCardell tackled the line again. He changed it to "While the wheels are whirring smoothly along a perfect track." The editor was satisfied, and they got paid thirty dollars for their work. That was the start of an association that lasted several years.

When Outcault moved out to Long Island, the poet and the artist saw less and less of each other. Partly because the comic strip artist spent more time reading law, medicine, Marcus Aurelius, Plato and Epicurus. This was part of his creative procedure. He thought of a funny picture, drew it and then made up some lines to fit it.

Outcault was working on the not-too-successful Por Li'l Mose when John Golden, up and coming Broadway producer, presented his children, Dick and Mary Jane, with a brindle bull terrier named Tige. The mischief the dog got the children in gave the artist an idea. He shuffled over to his drawing board, picked up a pencil and started to work. He pictured a small boy, a girl, and a chunky dog. The strip inspired by members of his own household was called Buster Brown and first appeared in the *New York Herald* on May 4, 1902.

The comic strip caught fire and Outcault developed a story, largely autobiographical, about a noisy, stunt-crazy household in the suburbs. Buster, in a high-starched collar and knee pants, usually stole the show and became one of the countless characters who influenced the lives of a large body of American readers. One of the early comics showed him jumping into a bath tub and turning the faucet on faster. Then he called the dog: "It's fine. Come in." Tige did with a big splash. Pretty soon the room was flooded. Buster, who led a hectic life, wound up his activities with a pillow tied to his posterior.

Other comic artists took a back seat when Outcault got going in high gear. The Katzenjammer Kids, long a leader in funny paper circulation, got off the front page of the colored section for the pranks of Buster Brown. The pace of the strip was fast. Buster and Mary Jane attracted millions of child readers, Mrs. Brown drew the women readers, and Mr. Brown, who took concealed delight in Buster's pranks, provided the paternal interest. At first they were the only characters, then a short, elderly woman wandered in one day and Buster said to her: "Pa's going to give me five dollars if you don't stay, Grandma, and I need the money." Grandma created a scene and muttered to her daughter as she headed toward the door: "I will cut you out of my will. You will never see me again."

Buster was much more refined than the Yellow Kid, yet Outcault could not keep reformers and educators off his neck. In 1905, when he went back to the *New York Journal,* their campaign to eliminate funnies from the newspapers reached full intensity. Their protests worried the gray-eyed artist from Lancaster, Ohio. He decided to close each comic strip with a moral in contrast to none in the Yellow Kid. Close followers of his strip began to note the preaching of Christian Science, founded by Mary Baker Eddy, in nearly all of Buster's resolves.

Whatever the origin of his preachings, Outcault's comic strip surpassed the popularity of

his earlier ones because he kept the epigram-
matical humor of the Browns intact, allowing
nobody to divert him from Buster's tricks. Take
Buster, for example, when he tried to fool Aunt
Emeline. He left his clothes on the bank of a
swimming hole and hid behind a clump of
bushes to make her think he was drowned.
"Ouch Tige," he exclaimed, "there's bumble bees
here. Get my clothes and we'll go away."

Tige: The clothes are gone, Buster.

Buster: Ouch, a bee stung me!

As Buster ran across a field, with horses
looking on in surprise and three girls covering
their faces, he caught up with the farmer who
stole his clothes. His resolution reveals how
Outcault put lessons into funnies: "That the loss
of my clothes does not worry me. To lose one's
self respect is the only serious loss. Clothes are
nothing. Character counts. I didn't fool my
Aunt Emeline. I fooled myself. That's what
always happens. Don't try to fool people. Try
not to fool 'em — that's the way to win." No
longer did Outcault try to kid his readers as
he did when, after the bathroom scene, Buster
remarked, "That I will never take another bath
as long as I live unless the Board of Health
interferes."

Buster Brown became a fad, and the artist

a creator of public taste. Not only were boys' styles set by Buster, but boys were even given his name. Girls wore huge bows in their hair because Mary Jane did every Sunday. Mothers used hairbrushes on their boys when they deserved a spanking because Mrs. Brown did, and fathers read the funnies to their tots if they did not lose betting on Buster Brown at the race tracks.

Outcault often pulled a prank himself to see whether or not it would be suitable for the comic strip. For months the people of Flushing whispered that the big house at 145 Madison Street was haunted. Strange noises came from the house at night and people stayed off the street. Keeping up the ghost was too boring, however, and Outcault gave up playing the piano in the deserted house at five o'clock in the morning. And he never used it as a situation in the comic strip.

He was a canny businessman, too. He had given away the rights to Yellow Kid trademarks, but now he demanded his share for the use of the Buster Brown name in suits, shoes, cigars, garters, stockings, belts and sweaters. He engaged a lawyer and two secretaries to look after his business interests, and his annual income soared over $75,000. He had so much money in a Flushing bank that none of the depositors understood how it could keep him from becoming a director.

In addition to his comic strips, he wrote and illustrated a number of Buster Brown adventure books, the first of which appeared in 1904. For the next nine years he turned out an average of two books a year, and his royalties from *Buster Brown Abroad, Buster, Mary Jane and Tige* and other books were larger than his comic strip income. As one title suggests, he traveled in foreign lands and sold Buster Brown trademarks for souvenir spoons from Singapore and scarahs from Egypt. He also collaborated on a Buster Brown play.

Although he was lionized as the creator of Buster Brown, and was asked to go on chalk-talk tours, Outcault proceeded with unusual caution. He hadn't forgotten the time years ago when Oscar Hammerstein, well-known theatrical producer, arranged for him to give a chalk talk in a New York variety show. He came out on stage, drew a picture of the Yellow Kid, and turned to face the audience. The silence spoke louder than words, and the curtain men rushed to their places. "W-w-well, t-that's the w-w-way it w-was," he stuttered.

It was no easy matter to persuade him to

give blackboard talks when Buster Brown was a big success. At last he consented. This time he began his first lecture out of town, in Wilkes Barre, Pennsylvania, and got over his stage fright. Somewhere along the lyceum circuit he met Frank Pershing, brother of the honored General Pershing, who proposed an advertising company to peddle the artist's pen and ink creations. They formed a partnership in Chicago, but Outcault was not long active when his son returned a war hero to take up the helm of the company.

He retired to devote himself to various pastimes. He painted portraits and outdoor scenes, but never for money. He gave away his oil paintings to friends. One of his favorite haunts was the Lambs, a swanky New York club open only to male members of the lively arts, and in his last years, when gray streaked his hair and flabbiness overtook his frame, he looked more like a sedentary banker than an artist.

The end came on September 25, 1928, and the remains of the man who brought out the first funnies went unsung to his grave. It is ironic. The funnies coaxed millions of Americans into the Sunday newspaper habit, yet the social commentators passed up Richard Outcault. He was a creator of public taste four decades ago, his Yellow Kid and Buster Brown have passed into our folklore, and he opened the eyes of advertisers, military leaders and propagandists to an effective means of communicating ideas. There's still a lot funnies can do. Outcault only fathered the way.

Chapter Ten

Father of the Labor Spies

In February, 1874, a red-haired, wiry young stranger with a heavy growth of beard entered the Indian Ridge mine near Shenandoah, then a rip-roaring mining settlement in Pennsylvania's coalland, and started to shovel coal into mine buggies. He handled the shovel clumsily, and stopped to lean on it often. Obviously he was not cut out for the work. The next day a delegate of the Miners' and Laborers' Benevolent Association, a tightly knit trade union of 30,000 members, demanded to see his union card.

"I hev no card to show ye," he replied in an Irish brogue.

"Unless you join our union," the delegate warned, "you will not be able to work in this mine."

The stranger soon realized that he could not take his task lightly, so when the delegate had gone he asked other miners how he could join the union. Not that he wanted to join, but he wanted to find out something about it and its officers. After work he pulled a shoddy gray waistcoat over a collarless flannel shirt, yanked a slouch hat over his hazel eyes, and roamed the town's innumerable saloons to pick up gossip about the miners' attitude toward their working conditions and employers. When the saloons closed, he knocked the ashes from his cutty pipe, stuck it into the faded band of his hat, and went to his room in Muff Lawler's boarding house. Then, after the Lawlers were asleep, he slipped downstairs to the cold kitchen and by the flickering light of a kerosene lamp wrote a report of everything he saw and heard. He put it in an envelope without a return address.

The letter looked harmless, but the stranger didn't think so. He carried only such writing materials that would not betray him, and for ink he used Mrs. Lawler's laundry bluing. He dared not keep the letter until the next day. He removed a stamp from a hidden slit in his hob-nailed boots and licked it on the envelope. Then, extinguishing the lamp, he walked steathily through the deserted streets to the post office and mailed the letter. Nobody would now trace it back to James McParlan, alias Jim McKenna, the new laborer at Indian Ridge Colliery.

The miners had no idea the stranger was introducing a new activity—labor spying—in labor-management relations. When the Pinkerton detective finally identified himself in a county courtroom a few years later, he let the labor movement in for enough trouble to keep their leaders on the alert ever since for signs of labor spies trying to cripple and discredit it. James McParlan, whose activities were front-page news in 1876 and 1906, was the first known and shrewdest of that secret band of labor spies who left a staggering trail of broken trade unions behind them as they swept across the land. The present crop of operatives, though forbidden by law to serve as labor spies, haven't allowed dust to be gathered on McParlan's methods.

His early years fulfill the popular picture of an agent provocateur. Born on a farm in Mullabrack parish, Armagh County, Ireland, in 1844, he left his Catholic parents at the age of nineteen to flit in and out of countless chemical works in England. Three years after, he tramped to Belfast, center of the Irish linen industry, to work in a warehouse.

He was not yet twenty-three when he left Ireland in 1867 to go to New York. The same year, after working as a delivery boy in a grocery store and clerk in a dry goods store, he headed for Chicago where he became a jack of all trades. Except for a brief spell in a Michigan lumber camp, he was successively a teamster, driver of a meat wagon, deck hand on a lake steamer, private coachman, bartender, proprietor of a liquor store and saloon. The saloon burned to the ground in the great Chicago fire of 1871 and left McParlan penniless. As a result of his experience as a guard for a Chicago detective agency, he landed a job with the famed Pinkerton Detective Agency, and with that agency he spent the rest of his days largely in industrial espionage.

About this time Franklin B. Gowen, newly elected president of the Philadelphia and Reading Coal and Iron Company, was beset with labor troubles. The miners' union was more of a threat to his autocratic power than any other element in the coal belt. In an attempt to discredit it, he charged that it hired outlaws known as Molly Maguires to take the lives of anyone who dared to work against its members. The name grew out of a legend that the ancestors of many Irish Catholic miners followed Molly Maguire, an Irish virago, when they fought evictions by English landlords in Ireland. Their mode of operation had some resemblance to the violence in the anthracite region, and presently all crimes were laid at the door of the Mollies. Allan Pinkerton, head of the first private-detective agency in the United States, undertook the job for Gowen of rooting out the Mollies.

To begin with, Pinkerton sent the young Irish detective into the haunts of the lawless coal miners. It took McKenna five months until he ingratiated himself with Muff Lawler, the Shenandoah saloon keeper who boasted of his authority over Irish Catholic miners, and then on the labor spy made each day's work just a little more interesting than the report he wrote the day before. No doubt he wanted to convince someone that it paid to employ him. All the reports, edited in the Pinkerton agency in Philadelphia, were delivered personally to Gowen. For spying on men who worked in Gowen's mines McKenna was paid $12 a week.

Despite his scorn of hard work, the cruddy from the Armagh bogs won the favor of the Mollies by his Irish wit and devil-may-care manners. He treated them to drinks with money he boasted he got from a counterfeit ring, and regaled them with tall yarns of his criminal activities in other localities. He looked upon cards, the bottle, songs, Irish jigs and women as accessories of his life. Some men kidded him, until rotgut whiskey caused his hair to fall out, that he might comb out his hair more oftener and drink less whiskey.

On April 14, 1874, a memorable day in his

life, McKenna, on his knees in Lawler's bedroom, took the oath of membership in the Ancient Order of Hibernians from Lawler, the bodymaster of the Shenandoah division. The members of this Irish Catholic secret society were out to promote friendship, unity and true Christian charity among themselves. Naturally the persecution and discrimination of Irish immigrants in remote coal towns, where it was more obvious than in large industrial areas because mining was about the only source of employment, struck the Hibernians to the bone. They sought to redress grievances.

With McKenna's advent into the secret society, there arose a factional strife as intense as a prize fight, and within three months he was elected secretary of the Shenandoah division. Now he was able to meet and compile a list of members of the fraternal order, and he didn't have to work in the mines anymore to learn what the rowdiest miners were up to. From that time the discord begun in Shenandoah spread to other divisions in Schuylkill and adjacent counties.

During these months Gowen had been expanding his domain. By the beginning of 1875 he locked horns with the union and vowed, "I'll turn Schuylkill County into a howling wilderness before I give in to the miners." From the spy reports Gowen knew just what the strikers would do, particularly in and around Shenandoah, and in May formed the Coal and Iron Police, a body of uniformed guards under Pinkerton's Captain Robert J. Linden, to work closely with McKenna. It is not strange, therefore, that Gowen chose this coal mining town to which to import a trainload of strikebreakers under the escort of his black-coated guards. The Coalies, as they were nicknamed, could foretell every movement of the strikers because a labor spy, with two revolvers in his belt and a big hickory club in his hand, was in their lines. The strikers, half-starved, demoralized and fighting among themselves, finally wavered. The strike collapsed. The union disintegrated.

But violence was not quite over. There was a sudden increase in murders as soon as McKenna shifted his interest from the labor scene to the cliques within the Ancient Order of Hibernians. There are two explanations for this phenomena. One group claims that some miners became desperate under the driving, blustering, power-mad Gowan; another group contends that McKenna set up crimes and charged them to the Mollies.

In any case, talk of marking offenders for

death came up more and more in body meetings, and one body asked another over the mountains to furnish strangers for intended crimes. Suddenly on the morning of July 6, 1875, Benjamin F. Yost, chief of police in nearby Tamaqua, was shot while putting out a street lamp near his home. McKenna received orders to investigate the murder and lay the groundwork for the arrest of the murderers.

Then, one day late in July, after his arrival in Tamaqua, McKenna stopped in at Jimmy Kerrigan's home to talk to Kerrigan, body-master of the Tamaqua division, about some affairs of the organization. McKenna turned the conversation to guns. Kerrigan brought out a black-handled thirty-two and handed it to McKenna. "That's the gun that kilt Yost," he said with a whiff of whiskey on his breath. McKenna controlled his countenance. He was an exuberant person, but he had developed a certain way of drawing out information.

"I guess you're wanderin' a bit, there!" McKenna said, "fur isn't it currently reported that Barney McCarron, Yost's own partner, shot him, because of a recent quarrel they'd had?"

"Oh! that's a swate enough story!" Kerrigan retorted, "but you'll allow that I know some-thin' of a job that I planned be myself, an' wor there on hand, when it wor all done!"

That night on the hill overlooking the tail of Panther Valley Kerrigan had another talk with the Pinkerton operative. Kerrigan had already told him the part he played, but McKenna, away from eavesdropping ears, had some other business to do. "I'll never brath a single word of it," Kerrigan confided as they parted at midnight.

Next day, after talking to the chief of the coal and iron police about Kerrigan's confession, McKenna decided to cultivate an intimate companionship with the Tamaqua miner through his sister-in-law, Mary Ann Higgins, whom he had met some months before at a Polish wedding in Shenandoah. He was dressed up like a duke of Chicago when he called for the sake of the Molly secrets he might wheedle out of her.

"What a pity she is of such a family!" he soliloquized. "And to think that I must get her brother-in-law hanged! Oh, I never can hope to have Miss Higgins transformed into Mrs. McParlan! Brother-in-law to a murderer! No! Never!"

While courting the girl in a free-and-airy style, he began to work with the Tamaqua Mollies on a plot to murder a mine boss named

John P. Jones in Lansford. McKenna agreed
to take two gunmen and himself to Lansford
to add Jones to the long list of murders. At the
last minute, however, he broke his promise. He
testified after that he went ahead of two gunmen to warn the intended victim and to alert
the Coalies. Yet on the morning of September
3, 1875, Kerrigan and two accomplices from
Schuylkill County, lying in wait, halted Jones
on the platform of the Lansford railroad station
in Carbon County and fired on him. With
apparently no warning of coming death, the
mine superintendent cried "I'm shot! I'm shot!"
and his body slumped to the platform.

Following a devious route over the mountains, Kerrigan led his companions to the spot
where he recently had a secret rendezvous with
McKenna and told them to wait until he went
home to get food and drinks. When he returned
to the woods, the men who were watching his
house closed in on him and his hungry pals.
The three were taken to Mauch Chunk jail to
await trial.

McKenna hastened to the seat of Carbon
County when Michael J. Doyle, one of the trio,
went on trial. No one paid any attention to
him, and he was free to go where he pleased
without publicity. Doyle was found guilty and

sentenced to the gallows. So was the next defendent, Ed Kelly. Somewhere along the route McKenna persuaded Kerrigan to turn state's evidence in order to save his neck.

Soon afterwards the wholesale arrest of Mollies in Schuylkill County raised a feeling in the society that they held a traitor in their midst. Who was he? McKenna threw suspicion off himself temporarily by quarrelling with Linden in a Shenandoah saloon, but he realized he was suspected definitely when Frank McAndrew, Lawler's successor as bodymaster of the Shenandoah body, discussed it when they walked together to the Pottsville court house.

"Some of the boys were making bets on the cars that you are a secret spy, a detective!"

"Me a spy?" exclaimed McKenna indignantly. "I will thank ye to name the man who dares to insult me by saying so!"

"Jack Kehoe!" responded McAndrew.

Kehoe, the most influential Molly in the county, realized the Mollies' peril and demanded McKenna's instant death. A few words with regional priests convinced McKenna that the Mollies knew all about him. He vanished. Not until five Irishmen charged with the murder of Yost were brought to trial in May did McKenna show up in the region again. For the first time he took the witness stand and revealed his identity as a Pinkerton detective. The story that F. B. Gowen had a Pinkerton labor spy, coal and iron police, and a lot of money behind the trial to prosecute the defendants grabbed the nation's headlines at the time.

With a combination of Kerrigan's fraudulent testimony, McParlan's undercover work, and mass hysteria, Gowen managed to send twenty Mollies, some guilty, some innocent, to the gallows. Surrounded by bodyguards, McParlan worked with the prosecuting lawyers until Kehoe received the death sentence, when he returned to his headquarters in Chicago with a feather in his russet toupe. There he married a neighbor's daughter, Mary Fitzgerald, and settled down to a life of comfortable ease. Tragedy struck twice, however, when his wife died in childbirth, and the girl born at the time died six years later.

In the meantime, William A. and Robert A. Pinkerton, who took over the detective agency in 1884 following their father's death, sent McParlan on a tour of their establishments. The terror of evil doers found that the superintendent of the Denver branch was grafting money from the Pinkerton agency. As a reward for his work William A. Pinkerton fired the superintendent and promoted McParlan to the head of the Western division.

McParlan directed its activities all the way to the Pacific. His men chased cattle rustlers, train robbers, claim jumpers, forgers, murderers, counterfeiters and outlaws. During a lull in activities, in 1887, he returned to the strident city on Lake Michigan and in a friend's home met an attractive blue-eyed girl from Princeton, Wisconsin. Her name was Mary Regan, and she was 32, when they were married on May 10, 1888. They went to Denver and lived in a beautifully furnished home, a bit of a sacrifice for a $45-a-week-man.

From all accounts he was a gentlemen by instinct, pleasantly mannered, a very religious man, very generous to the Catholic Church, and mild until aroused, and then he became a human Mt. Vesuvius. He saved all the energy he could for his agency. "Mary," he'd say to his wife, "exercise your good eyes for me, so I can save mine for business." She would then get a copy of Charles Dickens, his favorite author, and read to him from "Barnaby Rudge" or "Old Curiosity Shop."

Sometimes it seems McParlan did not stop to consider the motives for his deeds. Like a soldier, he yielded to the rules of the Pinkerton organization. He obeyed the demands which the superiors put upon him, for he realized that he could not disobey them without loss of position, property, and even life. To him obedience was better than sacrifice, and consecration to duty gave him new aims and purposes to enlarge the service of detectives or labor spies to employers. His duties ranged from labor spying to electioneering.

One of his first clients, for example, was Edward O. Wolcott, Republican candidate for U. S. Senator from Colorado. On election day McParlan detailed his operatives to various precincts. In each precinct, one detective went to the polling place while the other visited a saloon where he lined up citizens and took them to vote. The first dick would hand each voter a Wolcott ballot and guide him to a ballot box. Then the second one would drive the voters back to the saloon and hand each one a two dollar bill. Needless to say, Wolcott won.

But obedience to duty counted heavily. During the next election the Democrats engaged the Pinkerton men to do the same work for them as they did for Wolcott. McParlan never batted an eyelash. He told Charles Siringo, who participated in the aforementioned incident, to affect the costume of a hobo. "I voted eight times, as per McParlan's orders," said Siringo, "three times before the same election judges. For each vote I received 25 cents. Of course, I had to turn over this tainted money to my agency."

McParlan never talked much about his work. The most striking of his attributes, as one delves into his extraordinary career, was his grim silence about labor espionage in breaking up unions. He employed the same tactics of spying in the warfare between the hard-rock drillers and the mine owners of Colorado, Montana and Idaho as he did in Pennsylvania's hard coal fields. It was at about this time that he hired a young stenographer, Morris Friedman, to type for him. From this Russian immigrant, who was McParlan's stenographer from 1902 to 1905 and who wrote a book on his findings, *The Pinkerton Labor Spy*, the labor world learned more about McParlan's methods than the Molly Maguires ever did.

Now that he was easily recognized, he used little known operatives to carry out his cunning schemes. One of them, A. W. Gratias, Operative No. 42, was sent to Cripple Creek, Colorado, when the miners in that field downed their tools to cut off the supply of ore to striking Denver smelting mills. Gratias followed McParlan's example in Shenandoah.

Within a few months Gratias was appointed chairman of the local relief committee. McParlan now wrote him to make the relief bills as high as possible — and Operative No. 42 did, as high as $1,000 a week. The drain on the union's treasury was heavy, and in June, 1904, when the Western Federation of Miners convened in Denver, William D. Haywood, its one-eyed secretary-treasurer, objected to the large relief bills.

McParlan then instructed Gratias to cut relief as low as possible to starve the miners, and while doing this, to throw the blame on Haywood. It was done so cleverly that Haywood did not know about it until he read the letters between McParland and his operative in *The Pinkerton Labor Spy*.

Even before the strike failed, the hard-rock drillers of the Rocky Mountain region knew the Denver chief of the Pinkertons was back of several attempts to cripple their union. George H. Shoaf, a young, red-cheeked reporter for *The Appeal to Reason*, Socialist weekly, even suspected that McParlan wanted to assassinate him. With Vincent St. John, a chunkier and heavier miner though both stood about five feet and nine inches tall, Shoaf tried for several weeks to get a shot at McParlan, but the detective knew his stuff. He had a hack stop directly in front of the Miners Exchange Building, on Champa Street, in which he had his office. Under guard, he entered the hack, and on arriving home he emerged under guard. So long as he lived he had Pinkerton bodyguards to protect him.

Three weeks after the murder of Frank Steunenberg, an ex-governor of Idaho, by a bomb placed in the front gate of his home, McParlan entered a case that was to earn him this label: dean of black sleuthdom. The murder was traced to small, red-faced Harry Orchard, but he would not confess. On January 21, 1906, when state authorities placed him in charge of the investigation, McParlan said that Orchard was the tool of the inner circle of the Western Federation of Miners and then began to soften the murderer to his point of view.

Soon afterwards, in the state penitentiary at Boise, the two men had lunch together, and McParlan handed Orchard some expensive cigars. McParlan read to him from the Bible and told him that he intended to get him better quarters than the solitary cell he occupied. The prisoner had no reading matter and no visitors except McParlan.

"Harry," he said softly as he was about to

leave one day, "what is your mother going to think about this fix you're in?"

"What do you know about my mother?" Orchard asked anxiously.

"I know all about her," said the detective, knocking the ashes from his cigar, "and about your brothers and sisters, too."

McParlan left the jail. Orchard gradually began to think about what the detective had said. When the Pinkerton chief returned, Orchard admitted the crime and alleged he had been paid to commit it by officers of the Western Federation of Miners. Whereupon McParlan engineered the trap to catch Charles H. Moyer, president of the federation, George Pettibone, a former member of the executive committee, and Big Bill Haywood. All were arrested in Colorado without warrants and whisked away in a special train to Boise. The federation immediately engaged Clarence Darrow as legal counsel for the arrested men.

McParlan realized that Orchard's confession alone would not be enough to convict Moyer, Pettibone and Haywood. To corroborate Orchard's story, the Denver mastermind found Steve Adams, a miner who took part with Orchard in other crimes, and had him arrested on his uncle's ranch in Oregon and brought to

Boise. Somehow Adams signed a confession in a hurry. Only prison guards and McParlan were allowed to see the state's key witnesses.

There was one exception, however. Ethel Barrymore, an actress traveling through Boise with a road company, wanted to see Orchard out of curiosity. After appealing in vain to the governor and other state officials, she eventually came face to face with McParlan. Her appeal softened the detective visibly. On the way to the penitentiary, in a handsome carriage, the Denver man beckoned his bodyguard aside and gave him orders to let the actress see Orchard.

Which was more than Darrow could do. The jailor flatly refused to allow the defense attorney to see Orchard's cellmate. "I have my orders from McParlan," he said. "No one is to talk to him."

"But it's all right for McParlan and Barrymore to see Orchard, but not for me to see Adams," Darrow remarked. "Who hands out justice in Idaho?"

All attempts to secure permission from state officials being futile, Darrow called upon his long experience in criminal cases to pull a trick out of his bag. As a result Adams wrote a statement in the presence of his wife, who smuggled it out of the prison and made it public. It charged that McParlan forced him to corroborate Orchard's story and asked for his release.

Fuming, McParlan charged out of his suite in the Idanha Hotel and rushed to the prison. He handcuffed Adams and took him 300 miles north to Wallace, in the Coeur d' Alenes, to await trial for the murder of a claim jumper. Darrow cooled his heels again. The case ended in a hung jury, however, and Idaho had to go ahead with the trial of Haywood.

During the Boise trial, McParlan stuck close to his elegant suite and entertained newspaper correspondents with "red licker." He seldom left the Idanha Hotel except to coach Orchard how to act in the witness stand, for the prosecution, including Idaho's noted Senator, Bill Borah, hesitated to call him as a witness. It respected Darrow's power of cross-examining witnesses, and in the final plea to the jury Darrow turned upon McParlan with all the English at his command.

For hours Darrow continued his impassioned plea to the jury, yet McParland did not hear a word of it directly. Probably no man was painted as McParlan was that day in Boise. The jury returned with the verdict of acquittal for Haywood, and McParlan was barely able to stand it all. He began to turn into a wraith of his old distinguished self. No longer was there the proudly held head of an invincible detective, the shining face with bristling walrus mustaches, the beer barrel paunch. Denver saw a decrepit, skulking figure return from the war of entrapping bodies.

Wherever he went, he always watched out for an assassin's bullet. The eyes were hollow behind Horace Greeley spectacles, the cheeks rutted with worry, and the mustaches drooping like weeping willows. His paunch sagged. On May 18, 1919, at the age of 75, he breathed his last in Mercy Hospital. His church lodge conducted the funeral ceremonies and accompanied him to his last resting place. His grave in Mt. Olivet Cemetery outside Denver bears no epitaph.

Chapter Eleven

Father of Skyscrapers

If it had not been for the findings of a committee of outstandiig architects in 1932, the name of William Le Baron Jenney wouldn't mean much today. This committee learned that the Home Insurance Building, a twelve-story structure which Jenney designed in Chicago and which was razed about twenty years ago to make way for a 42-story office building, was the world's first true skyscraper. Until then every architect in the country who had designed a taller building claimed that he was the father of skyscrapers, and it is still amusing to read their claims in books tucked away in dusty corners of our public libraries.

If you looked through the portraits of all claimants, you could hardly find anyone who seemed less like the father of skyscrapers than Jenney. A person of medium height, with sandy hair combed to the side in an unruly manner, he didn't look the least bit like an architect. If he were pointed out on the main street of Chicago as a French art student, nobody would have been surprised. As a new-comer he still looked like a gay American in Paris, with a slender body thrown into an old brown suit that appeared to be older than his adopted city. His pale blue eyes were set in heavy bags of flesh that were obvious symbols of his lively student days in France.

One of the stories circulated about him was that, in the 1850's, he was known as a Yankee bon vivant at the Ecole des Beaux, the fountain-head of architectural education in France. One day he walked all over Paris looking for pumpkin pie. Nobody heard of the favorite American pastry. Finally he persuaded Madame Busque, owner of a little creamery in the Rue de la Michandiere, to try making it from a recipe he gave her. Madame Busque, who under-stood his French less than such struggling art students as James Whistler and George Du Maurier who frequented the dining room with Jenney, came out of the kitchen with the pumpkin prepared in a tureen. Then Jenney realized his mistake. He forgot to mention the crust, and the French proprietress immediately rolled out some dough and changed the mix-up from soup to pie.

When he landed in Chicago in 1868, he had a vast though oddly scattered curiosity in unusual structures. But the prospect that beckoned to him at thirty-five, just beginning to master design, color, form and ornament, was one that puffed the flesh under his eyes larger than teabags. His lips were compressed with the sadness of a man who had landed in the wrong place and refused to sleep until he got out. "He spoke French with an accent so atrocious that it jarred my teeth," commented a contemporary, "while his English speech jerked about as though it had St. Vitus' dance."

He tugged at his straggly Van Dyke beard and wrinkled a high forehead at the sight of ramshackle office buildings with small entrances, narrow hallways, and dark rooms. He quickly forgot the hopelessness of changing the architectural style of the jerry-built flats on the edge of a boundless prairie after an unruly cow kicked over Mrs. O'Leary's milking lamp in 1871.

The great fire left a vast area waiting for a new type of edifice. Chicago didn't care which type it got, for it was unhampered by traditions and codes. It was young and daring, and wanted to replace disheartening chunks of charcoal and piles of burned out clay with new buildings. Jenney stepped forward to show his plans. They were not just conglomerations of forms and materials. He wanted buildings to speak well of the way they were built and the materials of which they were made. His buildings, creating a bold adventurous skyline, pushed into the disdainful company of dirty ruins.

One of those ruins faced him in 1883 when he was commissioned to prepare designs for a tall fireproof building at Adam and La Salle Streets. His instructions from the Home Insurance Company, with headquarters in New York, were to design a ten-story building similar to other buildings he had designed in the previous decade. In his buildings, notably the Portland Block and the Leiter Building, he provided the maximum number of well-lighted small offices. The entrances were attractive. The halls were commodious and light. But Jenney was troubled. He could not provide these features in the new building without thinking about the greater load in the upper stories.

As he mulled over the problem, he remembered seeing in the Philippines bamboo huts which were built on a framework of four trees. The natives provided rooms by weaving smaller bamboos and leaves with the skeleton sides. Why couldn't he substitute iron columns instead of bamboo to achieve the same result? He found that he could use a metal skeleton, consisting of girders, beams and columns, to support all internal and external loads and carry all stresses directly to the foundations. He drew up the plans and presented them to the building committee of the Home Insurance Company. The committeemen looked at one another pop-eyed and then the chairman turned to the 50-year-old architect: "Where is there such a building?"

"There isn't any," Jenney replied, "but your building at Chicago will be the first."

"How do you know it is good?"

"Don't take my word for it. Take these designs to any bridge engineer you want, and ask him for his opinion. As you can see, the designs for the skeleton building resemble, in many respects, iron railroad bridges standing on end, side by side."

The committee let it go at that, and in March, 1884, Jenney received a building permit. In no time at all skilled engineers were on his neck. They said that expansion and contraction of the metal skeleton would push out the walls and kill all the people in the building, and some-one wanted to bet Jenney that it would topple over in the first stiff gale. For a while he heard agitation to prevent the erection of the towering structure. But he had too much to do other than to pay attention to head shaking.

He liked to get out, as he said, on the job. When the building was going up on the corner of Adams and La Salle streets, he climbed the scaffolding or catwalks as if he were the actual boss on the job. In those days the architect was a lord of construction. He directed the work skyward. But city officials finally butted in. They ordered him to fill the interior of cast-iron columns with concrete. Some years later the iron columns were a source of embarrassment to salvage men who, without knowing the columns were filled with cement, bought them on a pound basis.

When the iron framework reached the sixth floor, Jenney received a letter from Carnegie-Phipps, Pittsburgh rolling mill operators, with news of the first Bessemer steel beams and asked his permission to substitute them for wrought-iron beams on the remaining floors. He consented, and in appreciation the first processors of Bessemer steel named a lake ore freighter in his honor.

When the first tenants moved into the ten-story building (two stories were added later) in the fall of 1885, Chicago took on a new look. Facing La Salle Street the building, with two large banks on the first floor behind a granite front, looked impressive. The upper facade of the building was done in red brick with heavy stone belt cornices and the full length of the street front at the fifth, eighth and tenth floors. There were also stone window sills and lintels, with occasional brick pilasters in the corners of the facade to make up the architectural design.

The inside of the building was the most exciting part, for there Chicagoans got their first dose of vertical living. Two metal elevators, operating in a shaft hundreds of feet in height, took executives and young clerks up in the morning to open numerous places of business one upon another. Each shelf was divided by partitions into uniform compartments, and the elevators, privately controlled, served as a vertical thoroughfare. Elevator operators, who took certain people from the street and returned them to the street after they transacted their business in the skyscraper, became a new occupation, and "Call your floor, please" a new salutation. During lunch hours, the office beauties could be seen hurrying to the powder rooms which accompanied the modern plumbing facilities and then going down in an elevator for a snack in the sandwich shop on the street floor.

Their bosses showed up next door in their shirt-sleeves for a shave and haircut.

As the day wore on, the building, gilded by the rays of the setting sun, took on new color. By late afternoon less and less people passed in and out of this great gateway of commerce and secretaries turned to last-minute correspondence. Yet other secretaries locked valuables in their tile vaults—another new feature—until they returned the next day. Then came the last flow of traffic — office workers leaving the myriad-windowed building in the deepening gloom of night.

The building created nation-wide comment and established the use of skeleton construction for high buildings. It was America's greatest contribution to architecture. It enabled cities to expand upward in the area where they did the most business and thereby affected the value of downtown real estate. It placed a thousand people on a piece of land which formerly held only a few hundred. Jenney's brainchild resulted in the most brilliant era of structural engineering ever witnessed in the world.

Since then Chicago, New York, Los Angeles, Detroit and other cities have throbbed constantly with the staccato hammering of riveters high up on scaffoldings as new structures soared higher into the air. The skyscrapers multiplied so fast that a building stealing the sky one year was likely to be a toy the next as another site suddenly became ensnared in a giant network of steel and concrete. Today there are more than 5,000 buildings higher than the original Home Insurance Building. People still travel hundreds of miles to see the architectural wonders of our age.

What there is to see is amazing. Philadelphia has a bank that is taller than any other building in the city. Chicago has a church with its steeple 569 feet in the air. New York has a glittering panorama of towering steel and concrete, but nothing fascinates visitors as much as the Empire State Building.

Although Jenney's building set off a revolution in all of the structural arts and sciences, he took things as they came. He moved his office to the top floor of the new skyscraper and continued to turn out designs for other buildings. Presently, the bearded architect found himself in court at Chicago impatiently listening to the charge of a Minneapolis architect, Le Roy S. Buffington — to wit, infringement of letters patent on steel-frame construction. Jenney, who was as effusive as a Mexican jumping bean, bounced out of his seat without waiting for his lawyer to speak. "I am not guilty," he sputtered, and that ended the matter as far as he was concerned. Buffington's claim was never sustained in the courts.

The impulse with which Jenney had done things also started him off on his chosen career. He was born at Fairhaven, Mass., on September 25, 1832. His father was in the whale-oil business in New Bedford when the world still read by the light of the sperm whale's fat. When young William was seventeen, and the California gold rush was the attraction of all young men, he left Phillips Academy at Andover to sail in one of his father's whaling vessels around the Horn to California. From there he went to the Philippines where he was so impressed with the possibilities of railroad building that he decided to return home and study engineering.

After three years at the Lawrence Scientific School in Cambridge, Mass., he sailed for Europe and entered the Ecole des Beaux Arts. There he learned to consider and judge an architectural plan as a musician would a piece of music. In a dusty atelier, for example, Whistler showed him one of his paintings in which his sister was seated at a piano and her little child playing on the floor. To Jenney the piano was so out of proportion that it looked as if it were falling over. "Hurry and put a fifth leg under that piano," he guyed Whistler, "or it will fall and smash the baby."

Upon his return to the United States in 1856, he used his fund of knowledge as an engineer in building the Panama Railroad across the Isthmus of Tehuantepec, but after a year went again to France and spent 18 months in additional study in art and architecture. He met Richard M. Hunt, first of American architects to study in Paris, who was employed in designing the Pavilion de la Bibliotheque, opposite the Palais Royal, and Hunt's designs were to influence him greatly in his career.

At the outbreak of the Civil War he returned to the United States and entered the Federal Army. During most of the war he served under General W. T. Sherman's command. As an engineer he surveyed battlefields and prepared maps for the use of Sherman's forces. Subsequently he became chief engineer of the Fifteenth Army Corps and accompanied Sherman on his march from Atlanta to the sea.

Somewhere along the route he met Brigadier General Vinton, who was a habitue at Madame Busque's, and they started swapping their experience. It seems that another officer who had lost his way and wanted to pass the rest of the night in Vinton's camp claimed that he had known him as a student in Paris. When Vinton failed to recognize him, he asked the officer, "Who was the funniest man we knew in Paris?" Promptly the officer replied, "Whistler." "All right," said Vinton, "take that empty cot; you are no spy!"

When he took off his major's uniform in 1866, Jenney did some engineering work in Western Pennsylvania, and probably some in Cleveland, for the following year he married Elizabeth H. Cobb, a tall, charming daughter of a Roman scholar who owned a printing business in the latter place. The year he moved to Chicago, he formed a partnership with Sanford E.Loring, a pioneer in the manufacture of terra cotta for fireproof buildings, but the appearance of the dark-lit buildings discouraged him. He arranged with the University of Michigan to start one of the first college courses in the country on architecture. He traveled to Ann Arbor, Michigan, with the thought: "I'm going to teach architecture until I'm certain there are enough men who know how to design buildings." But his course was soon interrupted by the demand for his architectural services occasioned by the Chicago fire.

Louis Sullivan, an architect who has also

been called the father of skyscrapers, recalled
that when, in 1875, he went to work for Jenney
there was enough work to keep five men and
a boy busy. In Jenney's absences, the young
draftsmen literally raised the roof off the place.
The 24-year-old foreman, John Edelmann, who
was left in charge, didn't help matters, either.
He usually jumped on top of a drawing table
and made a howling stump speech on social
reform. After Edelmann agitated the men,
Sullivan would quiet them with a song from
some oratorio, preceding it with the cry, "Ye
people, rend your hearts, but not your garments." The deviltry went on until someone
shouted, "Cheese it, Cullies; the boss!"

Sometimes the lithe, free-and-easy architect
pranced into the atelier like a trapeze artist who
had just seen the sight for a new skyscraper
from a high wire. Sometimes he lurched toward
the head draftsman in a hurry to see a new
design. The staff, half-mesmerized by the atelier
patron, found itself driven into an orgy of thinking about the refacing of the architecture surface. His understudies spoke of him, but never
to him, as "Papa." If he liked a student or a
draftsman in his office, he would stop his work
and spend an hour or two in the study of designing. As a result a number of young architects

obtained their first ideas of skeleton construction from him. Daniel H. Burnham, who headed the construction of the World's Columbian Exposition on 600 acres of sandy wastes on the southern shores of Lake Michigan in 1893, was one of his disciples. Other students were William Holabird, Martin Roche, and Dan Everett Waid.

Jenney was a familiar figure in Chicago's art clubs and eating houses. As a teacher, as a director of the American Institute of Architects, as a raconteur and as the pioneer of "Chicago construction" he was one of the best known citizens of the city. Whenever banquets were to be given in honor of some celebrity, and the committee felt shaky in its food and wine choices, it called upon Jenney. He was familiarly known as "Mr. Gourmet" among his friends.

His home in Riverside, a suburb west of Chicago, where he lived with his wife and two boys, was often filled with friends. He liked the spirit of small gatherings when friends came in and said, "What do you have on the charcoal grille tonight?" Invariably after work he brought home a variety of wild fowl, imported cheese and other delicacies. He was a hail fellow well met, an officer of the Loyal Legion, and one of the best authorities of James Whistler in Chicago.

For example, when they were discussing the peculiarities of Henry James and his habit of dragging a small incident through several pages, the waiter brought them each a glass of wine. Jenney tasted it and remarked, "The best of wine is spoiled by too small a spigot."

"What's that?" Whistler piped up. "What's that you said? Did you get that out of Shakespeare?"

"Not at all; it is simply a physical fact that if you let good wine dribble through a small spigot you lose its fragrance and character."

"God bless me," exclaimed Whistler, "but I believe you are right; and it's a good saying — it's James to a — drop."

In 1891, feeling that he wanted to take his work easier, Jenney formed a partnership with William B. Mundie, a clever Scotch-Canadian draftsman who had helped to make up the plans for the Home Insurance Building. They erected an imposing array of tall buildings in Chicago. Among them were the Siegel, Cooper & Co.'s department store, Union League Club, Y. M. C. A. Building, New York Life Insurance Building, the Horticultural Building at the World's Columbian Exposition.

The last design on which he worked was the Vicksburg Memorial, a gift of the people of Illinois in memory of their fallen heroes on the battlefield of Vicksburg. Unfortunately Jenney was too ill to attend the dedication and Mundie took his place. About that time Elmer C. Jensen became a partner, and the firm was known as Jenney, Mundie & Jensen. Jenney withdrew from the firm in 1905 and retired to Los Angeles, California, where he lived with his son Max. Two years later he passed away. Though he is forgotten today, the skyscraper stands as a fitting memory to his genius.

Chapter Twelve

Father of Labor Day

On the eighth evening of May, 1882, Peter J. McGuire, a sandy-haired, 29-year-old carpenter aglow with ideas, walked briskly along New York's Thirteenth Street and up a narrow stairway of a small building. Upon entering Clarendon Hall, where the recently formed Central Labor Union was meeting, he greeted a room as full with German socialists and Irish rebels as the spines on a porcupine's back.

"Mr. Chairman," he announced in a rich baritone voice as soon as the unfinished business was out of the way, "I wish to introduce a resolution."

"You have the floor, Pete," the chairman said.

"I propose," Pete continued, "that one day of each year be set apart to be designated as Labor Day — a general holiday for the laboring masses."

"Are there not enough holidays?" asked someone in the hall.

"We have numerous holidays, it is true,"

replied McGuire. "But they are all religious, or civil, or military. What I want is not so much a holiday as a day which shall be Labor's— an occasion devoted to the industrial spirit, the great vital force of every nation."

"Do you have a date in mind?" asked the chairman.

"Well," McGuire thought a moment, "we have the Fourth of July and then no break until Thanksgiving. What would you think of the first Monday in September? It would come at the pleasantest season of the year, and it would divide that long stretch."

In all the man-made holidays celebrated in the United States, none is more peaceful than Labor Day. Men, women and children enjoy it at the seashore, in parks and elsewhere. Yet Peter J. McGuire and his advocacy of Labor's Own Day remain virtually unknown to the overwhelming bulk of Americans. The last thought in their plans is a far cry from his reason for a holiday. Both the *Encyclopedia Americana* and the *Encyclopedia Britannica* give McGuire no credit for starting this holiday. He is one of the forgotten fathers in our growth as a nation.

Born on July 6, 1852, in the tenement district of cluttered fire escapes, washlines and crowded stoops of Lower East Side in New York, Peter James McGuire was marked for the enjoyment of life. His mother, Catherine, said to be an Irish-born niece of Dewitt Clinton, who opened the Erie Canal in his third term as Governor of New York, was a devout Catholic who had fourteen children, but eight of them had died. His father, John, was an Irish immigrant who worked in Lord and Taylor's department store. Peter was eleven when his father caught the war fever from watching a parade and enlisted in the Union Army, leaving his wife and five children without a large bank account.

Soon Pete, the eldest boy, had to quit school to help the family exchequer. He sold newspapers and blacked shoes on street corners. He held horses and swept out shops. He ran errands. "I was everything but a sword swallower," he remarked to friends in the last years of his life. "And sometimes I was so hungry, a sword — with mustard, of course — would have tasted fine."

On one occasion when working in Horace Greeley's office at the *New York Tribune*, he noticed the absent-minded editor mopping his face frequently with a handkerchief. Although the day was warm, young McGuire could not understand why Greeley would want to wipe his face and still work with his hat on. "Mr. Greeley," he said quietly, "I don't know what's the matter with your face but it's all yellow."

Greeley grunted, mopped his face again, and the telltale trace of yellow on the handkerchief reminded him of something. He yanked off his hat and there it was — a package of butter he had forgotten — almost melted away.

When the elder McGuire took off his war uniform, Pete followed him through the employes' entrance of Lord and Taylor's. After a full day's work in the department store he attended night school at Cooper Union, which was conceived by Peter Cooper as a center for the education of young people. It was there that he first met a young, black-haired cigar maker named Samuel Gompers, who like himself later became a founder of the American Federation of Labor.

At 17, Pete quit the department store to enter a piano factory as an apprentice to the cabinet-making trade. There the teachings of German wood joiners had a profound effect upon him. The cabinet makers' union was affiliated with the International Workingmen's Association, the organization founded by Karl Marx, and Pete joined both organizations in 1872 when he became a qualified carpenter.

The groups he joined were soon consuming most of his time. His union activities led him into the revolutionary movement. For the revolutionary movement, especially in those days, was carried across the Atlantic by dispossessed workers from various parts of Europe and was very closely allied to the communities of immigrants in New York. It attracted idealists of all kinds, and after union meetings, McGuire's tall figure was found in a circle of socialists in the old Tenth Ward Hotel, where far into night they would discuss the problems of labor. In P. J. McGuire, it found, wrote Gompers in his autobiography, "a fiery young orator with a big heart, and as yet immature judgment."

After the financial panic of 1873, McGuire became the most amazing soap-boxer New York had ever seen. Standing five feet nine and a half inches, muscular, with a small mustache and alert blue eyes, this carpenter looked like a regular Army drill sergeant. He always wanted to end up his orations with a parade, for he believed that it would publicly show the strength and esprit de corps of the masses.

The ward bosses of the Tammany ring did not like it when he led unemployed marchers down to City Hall to ask help from the Mayor

219

and Aldermen. Neither did his father who stood one Sunday on the front steps of St. John's Catholic Church and shouted from the top of his lungs that his eldest son had disgraced him.

Young McGuire's heart ached. This was hard to take. The streets were still filled with unemployed. Finally he settled upon a plan of attack.

He called a mass meeting of the unemployed for 11 A. M. on January 13, 1874, in Tompkins Square, in the heart of the tenement district. Its purpose was to present the mayor with a program of their demands. It was a revolutionary program — different from anything the country had seen. In it McGuire, the wayward son of a department store functionary, advocated, sixty years before Roosevelt's New Deal unemployment insurance and public works to provide jobs for the unemployed. At the last minute the police withdrew the permit to hold the meeting, and other unemployed leaders tried to persuade McGuire to call it off to prevent bloodshed.

"No," he replied. "We will hold it at 11 A. M. as set. This is a public square. We are the public."

Long before eleven o'clock the unemployed began to gather inside the high iron fence of

Tompkins Square. The wide gates were guarded by mounted police and patrolmen. With the sound of marching feet echoing up Avenue A, the atmosphere grew tense. At the head of the marchers was the king of parade makers, his soldierly step setting him apart from the rest as they approached Seventh Street.

When they got near the open gates, the police surged upon them from all sides, swinging their clubs. A throaty wail of anguish arose. Many heads were broken. McGuire was knocked to the ground. The excited crowd rushed backward, then scattered in confusion. McGuire got back on his feet and looked for someone to nurse his bloody wounds.

Thenceforth, he realized that workers had to take political action into their own hands to help themselves by producing goods under a cooperative plan instead of waiting for private enterprise. For the next six years he gave all his time, exceptional speaking ability, zeal and trobbing energy to establishing workers' political groups, winning members for the Lassallean party, and preaching the glories of the cooperative commonwealth. The depression was ripe for this kind of world — at least he thought so. Sometimes he ate only once a day in order to save enough to visit places in New England and the Middle West with his message. When he lacked funds, he turned to his trade, and continued campaigning in his spare time.

He succeeded with the help of other reformers to secure the passage of important labor bills in the Missouri legislature, one of which was the establishment of the Bureau of Labor Statistics. As deputy commissioner of this bureau in 1879, he became acquainted with the conditions of labor in Missouri and found a more serious problem to him than political reform. Something must be done about raising wages and shortening hours of work. He saw that betterment of working men must come primarily through collective bargaining.

He quit his post and went to work as a furniture worker in St. Louis. He worked hard and effectively to organize the carpenters in the St. Louis area and then formed a trades' assembly to unify the activities of local unions. Under his leadership the wages of carpenters rose within a short time from $1.50 to $3.00 a day. Encouraged, he issued a call for a national convention of carpenters to meet in Chicago. Consequently, on August 8, 1881, twelve carpenters' unions from scattered regions formed the United Order of American Carpenters and Joiners. McGuire was elected General Secretary, at a salary of seven hundred and fifty dollars a year.

He immediately got busy to weld the various groups of city assemblies, trade unions and dissatisfied Knights of Labor into a national organization known as the Federation of Trades and Labor Unions. He set up his headquarters in New York and started a journal, *The Carpenter*, to carry labor's message and his fight for the eight-hour day. But the crowning achievement of his life was the campaign he started in 1882 to gain Labor Day.

The first annual parade was not celebrated on the first Monday but on Tuesday, September 5, 1882, because the regular session of the Central Labor Union was held that day. More than 10,000 wood joiners, cigar makers, printers, bricklayers and other workers came out of the city's dark tenements and close-packed homes to march in the Labor Day parade. They sported their best Sunday clothes, smoked cigars and waved high top hats, canes, handkerchiefs as the parade headed up Broadway from City Hall to Union Square, the heart of the city's radical activities. There, around a reviewing stand lost in a field of banners which read: "Workers, Band Together," "Labor Creates All Wealth," and "Agitate, Organize, Educate," the big gathering heard an imposing array of speakers.

After that the trade unionists and their families, predominately immigrants from England, Ireland and Germany, went to Elm Park, farther uptown, to hold a picnic.

Although the entire affair brought people of different trades and tongues closer together, McGuire was not entirely satisfied. What about the rest of the country? As he traveled from city to city and state to state, thundering forth his slogan of eight hours for the workers, the Labor Day movement seemed to follow him. In 1884, when the Federation of Trades and Labor Unions met in Chicago, the delegates jumped on McGuire's bandwagon and sent a resolution to Washington urging Congress to declare the first Monday in September a national holiday.

Congressional leaders paid as much attention to their request as they did to labor's demand for creation of a national bureau of labor statistics and enforcement of the eight-hour law passed in 1868. Nevertheless, the blue-eyed carpenter from New York kept up the agitation. Finally, on February 21, 1887, the first law to make Labor Day legal was passed in Oregon. Within the next three months, in this order, Colorado, New Jersey, New York and Massachusetts passed similar laws. But McGuire's dream of a national holiday was still a long way off.

His crusade almost ended right after his marriage to Christina Wolff, a small, blue-eyed brunette from Staten Island, on October 6, 1884. With their things packed in preparation to leave New York to open new headquarters for the carpenters in Cleveland, McGuire went down to Justus Schwab's saloon to say goodbye to his friends. The sight of the labor leader in his best traveling clothes collected a rapt, admiring audience of cigar makers, teamsters and clothing workers around him. Johann Most, a well-known anarchist of medium height, sighed as he stood on the fringe of the crowd.

"Now that you're married, McGuire, perhaps you'll give up the cause and sell out the workers," Most said.

McGuire's eyes blazed. "I've never known what good you did the German workers when you tried to kill King Wilhelm I," he shot back. "Anarchy has never solved the workers' problems."

Most drew back to pull a gun out of his pocket, but before he had a chance to shoot, one of the workers stepped forward and grabbed his arm. Half an hour after the incident McGuire and his 25-year-old bride left New York City on a fast train. For the next four years they lived in Cleveland and then in Philadelphia. They moved frequently, as the family increased to three girls and a boy, because the carpenters' secretary sought some little improvement in comfort or rent.

In the meantime the Federation of Trades and Labor Unions that he and others had started in Terre Haute became, on December 8, 1886, the American Federation of Labor. Sam Gompers was elected president and McGuire, although he declined, secretary. The labor movement, sparked by the carpenters' campaign for the eight-hour day, then began to grow, develop and expand.

The carpenters were the leaders in the eight-hour day movement because, when it decided to concentrate activity in one trade each year, the A. F. of L. selected the Brotherhood of Carpenters to move for the eight-hour day. The rank and file carpenters of the Knights of Labor were asked to support a demonstration for the eight-hour day, but Terence Powderly, the head of the Knights, refused to have anything to do with it. Furthermore, he tried to kill the movement by saying a general strike would be called on May 1.

As time went on the pragmatic president of the A. F. of L. saw how he could widen the carpenters' drive. It occurred to him that the International Workingmen's Congress, which was to meet in Paris on July 14, 1889, could aid McGuire by an expression of world-wide sympathy from that congress. McGuire, an old hand at these congresses, was too busy at the time, so Hugh McGregor, who belonged to Die Zhen Philosphen with McGuire in the 70's, was sent to Paris to rally support. Despite some opposition, the Congress voted to hold a demonstration on that day in every country of Europe for the eight-hour day.

With the general winning of the eight-hour day, McGuire and American labor ignored May Day as a labor holiday. It became the day in which the workers of Europe articulated in celebrations the aims of socialism and a classless society. Very few American workers undertook mass demonstrations for these aspirations. McGuire, now first vice president of the American Federation of Labor, appeared in Washington to push labor bills in Congress and particularly his own idea for Labor Day.

Long experience with legislatures made him cagy and bi-partisan. It was smart to push the bills for which there was the most popular support. With 32 states already in favor of Labor Day in 1894, McGuire's first ray of hope came when Congressman Amos J. Cummings of New York City introduced H. R. 28 designating September's first Monday for the honoring of labor. The bill, however, was sent to the committee on labor and forgotten for a long time. McGuire went to work with renewed spirit, and in the next session Senator James H. Kyle, a former Congregational minister out of Aberdeen, South Dakota, earned McGuire's undying gratitude by introducing S. 730 which, although referred to the labor committee, brought out the earlier bill with a report of the House committee. The Senate concurred and on June 28, 1894, President Grover Cleveland proclaimed the first Monday in September a national holiday.

Congress summed up its action in these words: "By making one day in each year a public holiday for the benefit of workingmen the equality and dignity of labor is emphasized. Nothing is more important to the public weal than the nobility of labor be maintained. So long as the laboring man can feel that he holds an honorable as well as a useful place in the body politic, so long will he be a loyal and faithful citizen."

Labor Day is today a legal holiday not only

in the United States but also in Puerto Rico, Hawaii, Alaska and parts of Canada. Europe has stuck to the first of May since 1890 as Labor Day, but it is no longer a peaceful event. Russia has turned the official holiday into a military one by featuring mobile tanks and Red Star soldiers.

McGuire was pleased at the trend the observance was taking in the United States at the turn of the century. Labor celebrated its achievements and renewed its vows for the furtherance of its hopes. But what lay ahead for him was suffering and disillusionment because Congress bypassed the eight-hour day, forty-hour week, to go with it. He was unable to attend the A. F. of L. conclave in Louisville, Kentucky, in 1900, and thus had to give up his place as first vice president. It was plain to all who came in contact with him early in 1901 that McGuire had lost his health in the labor movement. His service over thirty years had drained his vitality. Then there was his specific malady — dropsy. In September, 1901, his personal physician ordered him to give up his remaining post with the carpenters' brotherhood, which paid him $2,000 a year. He could little afford to lose this income.

Gradually he lost all influence in the labor

movement and doctor bills, food and rent took all his savings. The bounty of friends was not enough to provide the essentials of life. The family was forced to move from a three-story house with a bay window and pleasant garden where he had moved in 1893 to a run-down house on Byron Street, on the Camden side of the Delaware River. "This is the end of me," McGuire murmured.

Soon afterwards his successor, Frank Duffy, who recently retired as General Secretary of the United Brotherhood of Carpenters and Joiners, paid him a call one day and asked, "Did you make your peace with God?"

"I never was at war with God," McGuire replied.

Not long afterwards he began to play a game of hands with his pretty 19-year-old daughter, Kathryn, who immediately noticed that he was trembling.

"Papa!" she cried. "What's the matter?"

"Baby, I'm frozen."

The family sent for the doctor and his diagnosis was erysipelas. For four days Kathryn and her sisters supplied cranberry poultices on his face, but McGuire wouldn't respond to treatment. On Sunday, February 18, 1906, the family sent for a priest to administer the Last

Sacraments, but when he arrived McGuire was dead. After his burial in Calvary Cemetery, his body was disinterred and transferred to Arlington Cemetery, in Pennsauken, four miles from Camden. Above his grave is a monument on which the motto of the A. F. of L., Labor Omnia Vincit, is carved. No epitaph better describes McGuire's crusade.

Chapter Thirteen

Father of the Coal Breaker

Hardly anyone in the anthracite region who bends over the iron-teethed rollers that crack the coal and the screens that sort it into various domestic sizes has ever heard of Joseph Battin. More than anyone else, Battin has left an indelible mark on the hard coal country in northeastern Pennsylvania with his invention of the coal breaker. His name should rank with James Hargreaves, Edward Cartwright and Eli Whitney, for his invention probably contributed as much to the industrial revolution as the spinning jenny, the power loom and the cotton gin.

So little is known about him that some writers continue an historical injustice begun long ago by referring to Gideon Bast instead of Battin as the father of the modern coal breaker. The facts are found in a few relatively obscure documents. Gideon Bast, one of the first operators in the Broad Mountain tract of Schuylkill County, owned Wolf Creek Colliery near Minersville where Battin erected the first machine for breaking and screening coal.

Joseph Battin had just turned thirty-seven

when he introduced the coal breaker that was to pile mine waste in many a miner's backyard in the next century. The son of poor Quaker parents, he was born on a farm just outside the western edge of the anthracite region, in Greenwood Township, Columbia County, on May 26, 1807. When still a boy, husky and powerful as a young bull, he came out of the highlands to look for a job in Philadelphia.

The Quaker city on the Delaware was the El Dorado of the mechanically inclined, for its ambition was to become the workshop of the world. Young Battin gradually worked himself up from obscurity until, in 1838, he received recognition for helping to build the Northern Liberties Gas Works in that city.

At that time gaslight was attracting increasing atention as a mode of illuminating streets, shops, dwellings and factories. Baltimore had gaslight as early as 1825, when coal was imported from England to manufacture coal gas. Rosin was also used, but it was not as popular as coal gas because it blackened walls and left an offensive smell. The Philadelphia plant is noteworthy because it was the first to extract gas from our own supplies of bituminous coal along the Monogahela, Allegheny and Ohio rivers. Joseph Battin played a major part in its success, for he licked one problem after another connected with the use of American bituminous coal. So successful was he that, in 1841, the Board of Managers of Northern Liberties elevated him to the post of superintendent of the gas works.

Battin possessed not only a knack for solving a mechanical problem, but an infinite capacity for creating new things. In his own shop, not far from the gas works, he had begun to perfect a machine for breaking and screening coal the year after he became superintendent. He knew there was need for such a machine because he had observed the crude methods of preparing anthracite for domestic use when he went through the coal fields on his way to visit his parents on the farm north of Bloomsburg.

Besides, he began his experiments for the most practical of reasons — he needed money. Since his marriage the first day of 1829 to Harriet Strong, he tried to surpass his father's progenitiveness of thirteen children. His first child was born the same year of his marriage and another followed regularly every two years until he counted six boys and four girls in the household.

In his efforts to perfect a labor-saving coal breaker, he set teeth opposite each other in the cast iron rollers. The way the teeth hit together, however, pulverized the coal sent through the rollers too much. Next he placed teeth in one roller in such a way that when it revolved the teeth would fit into the empty spaces between the teeth in the other roller. He turned the two rollers in opposite directions. The rollers, however, were not the most important parts in Battin's idea, for what he wanted was a machine to break and screen coal at the same time. So, on top of the rollers, he built a hopper for the coal to pass from the rollers to a long screen hung in an inclined position. The screen, the holes of which were made up of four or five sizes, sorted and cleaned the coal as it passed through the rollers.

Battin was now ready to apply for a patent. How could he get one? Taking out a patent was enough to befuddle the wits of any inventor. Nobody knew much about the patent system, for it was only seven years old when on September 11, 1843, he filed an application for a patent of his invention with the Patent Commissioner in Washington, D. C. Almost a month later, on October 5, 1843, he obtained the first patent ever issued in this country for a "coal-breaking machine." It was U. S. Patent No. 3292.

The Philadelphia inventor soon realized that

his first patent did not protect him very much. In it he claimed only the combination of a roller breaking machine with a screen for separating the coal into different sizes. He did not claim the manner of arranging and combining the toothed rollers, and for that omission he was to pay heavily in later years. Anyway, when he had made certain improvements in the arrangement of the toothed rollers, he applied for a new patent. That was in February, 1844.

In his second application he was more specific. The auxiliary roller, he said, "I sometimes used for the purpose of reducing such large lumps of coal as might not be readily acted upon by the principal rollers . . . I have found, by continued experiment, that such rollers constitute a real improvement in any breaking machine. . . ."

His claim, therefore, was actually for a new invention, and in doing so, he claimed an unprotected element of the coal breaker he patented in 1843.

Battin's first big chance to show the usefulness of the coal breaker came when Gideon Bast, one of the most indefatigable and successful pioneers in the corps of coal operators, asked him to set up the coal breakers at his colliery on Wolf Creek, north of Minersville. Gideon Bast, who was the first to apply steam power to mining, wanted to lessen the labor of preparing marketable coal, and by April, 1844, the Battin coal breaker was in operation at his place. The new breaker, run with a ten horse power steam engine, saved him the labor of at least sixty men. From then on more than 200 tons of coal a day were hauled away from Wolf Creek Colliery.

The success of Battin's breaker was so great that other operators hurried to sign agreements with him. The terms under which the breakers were built resembled a page of Stephen Girard's book. Girard, the Philadelphia financier who owned coal lands in Schuylkill and Columbia counties, leased them to coal operators on a royalty basis. Batin did the same with a royalty generally fixed at one cent a ton. With coal production rising at an astounding rate, he seemed to be on the road to riches.

In the midst of his early success, he met an English blacksmith named Benjamin Haywood, who in his pretentious machine shops in Pottsville had built a coal breaker in which one roll was fitted with teeth the same as in Battin's breaker and the other was perforated. When the rolls rotated, the teeth slipped into the holes and thus crushed the coal. On May 21, 1845, Haywood obtained a patent for this breaker, but eight months before that he assigned his rights to Joseph Battin under an unusual agreement. Battin was to pay him $200 for every so-called Battin-Haywood breaker he erected, and Haywood in turn was to become an agent for the duplex breaker.

The Haywood breaker was first put up at the old Lawton mine, on the west side of Mill Creek, north of Pottsville, where Haywood was one of three partners in Milnes, Haywood & Co. By acquiring the patent rights of Haywood's invention Battin now collected from the company two cents for every ton broken. Thereupon, according to the agreement, Battin paid the royalty to Haywood, not to the company.

The Battin-Haywood breaker, however, was not as good as the Battin breaker. The result was that Battin found himself building his breakers and very few, if any, of the Battin-Haywood breakers.

His virtual monoply in this field was not without its eventful headaches. His revenue grew so large that some coal operators began to skip monthly royalty payments to him, and still others began to infringe on his patent rights. Such action dragged him into both local and federal courts for years to come.

The first time he took a case to court he was

defeated. That was in April, 1847, when he sued John Clayton and Enoch W. McGinnis, partners in a coal mine near Pottsville, in a Pennsylvania circuit court to recover damages for infringement of his 1843 patent. The court decided that Battin could not uphold his suit because his first patent covered, the judged reasoned, merely the combination of machinery.

As a result Battin surrendered his patents of 1843 and 1844 and obtained a reissue of the 1843 patent upon an amended specification on September 4, 1849. The patent of 1844 was not reissued. Samuel Battin, the inventor's brother, was listed in the application as the assignee.

Now that they were fortified with stronger claims, the Battin brothers decided to push their claims to the highest courts. From their next action grew one of the most important legal cases in the history of the coal industry. In 1850, the Battins, in three separate cases, brought suits against James Taggert, Robert Radcliffe, John Johnson and John G. Hewes for not paying royalties under their patent rights. The defendants pleaded not guilty, and when they came up for trial, the jury returned a verdict in favor of Joseph and Samuel Battin. A new trial was granted, however, when the

defense lawyers claimed that they had un-
covered new evidence and had found descriptions
of old stone crushers in foreign publications
with which to argue the case.

The trial finally came up in the Pennsylvania
circuit court in October, 1852. The cases of the
four operators were argued and decided together. Judge John K. Kane presided. Although
each side had two lawyers, neither enjoyed the
privilege of seeing how their arguments affected
the jurors, for Judge Kane took charge of the
jury. He instructed the jury to return a verdict
for the defendants.

Judge Kane, in charging the jury, said: "Mr.
Battin's invention, as he now defines it, was in
use for nearly six years before he claimed that
it was his property. He had made it known as
an unprotected element of the combination he
patented in 1843. It was not until 1844 that
he asserted any other right in it for himself
than he conceded to everybody else. He cannot
reclaim what he has thus given to the public."

Joseph Battin was not the type of man to
take defeat lying down. He took the case to the
United States Supreme Court. Associate Justice
John McLean, 69-year-old native of New Jersey,
who sat on the Supreme Court bench from 1829
to 1861, delivered the opinion of the high

judicial body in the December term, 1854. Some of his remarks reveal the way the invention of Battin's breaker was enveloped in legal cobwebs. Said Judge McLean:

"The patent of 1843 was not surrendered on the obtainment of the patent of 1844. That was intended to be a new invention of arranging and combining the toothed rollers, which, the patentee says, was not made the subject of a claim in the patent of 1843. The patent of 1844 was cancelled, but not reissued, when the patent of 1849 was issued. At that time the patent of 1843, and the improvement thereon, dated January 20, 1844, were surrendered and cancelled, and new letters-patent were issued on an amended specification.

"We think the court also erred in saying to the jury, 'We instruct you that the verdict, in each case, must be for the defendants.'

"This . . . took from the jury facts which it was their province to examine and determine . . . they are to determine whether the invention has been abandoned to the public . . ."

In reversing the judgment of the Pennsylvania circuit court, the U. S. Supreme Court gave Joseph Battin the victory he long awaited. But it came just as the 15-year-limit of his patent rights were about to expire. Altogether the judicial contests over his claims cost Battin about $100,000.

If Battin thought he was through with legal battles, he had another thought coming. Benjamin Haywood, who had shipped a large number of prefabricated houses to California during the Gold Rush and gone out there in a vain attempt to sell them, returned to Pottsville about 1856 to enter the legal arena with Joseph Battin. He claimed that he had no return from his invention because Battin did not protect him in his exclusive right to make the breaker and that other persons were making and selling the Battin-Haywood breakers. Battin replied, but Haywood was insistent. He demanded compensation and damages from Battin amounting to $200 for every breaker embracing his and Battin's improvements.

In an exchange of letters, the feud between the two inventors rose to a fever pitch. It did not help Battin's relations with the coal owners, and in the end he offered to settle the matter by paying Haywood $1500 in three installments over a period of two years or $1000 in cash.

"Battin offers them," wrote his lawyer, William H. Rawle, "not because he has the least doubt of his ability to defeat the alleged claim, but that it is for his interest to settle all his difficulties with the coal region at the same time."

The case never reached the courts, for the men reached a mutual settlement.

It is interesting to compare this case to another in which Battin was the plaintiff. In March, 1867, he showed Henry Martin, then a resident of Bergen township, in Hudson County, New Jersey, a rough model of a machine for making bricks. Marin agreed to take the model, improve and perfect it, procure a patent for it, in his name, and share the profits with Battin.

Soon afterwards Martin disappeared, and it was not until 1899 when reading an advertisement in a trade journal that Battin located him in Lancaster, Pennsylvania, where he was selling hundreds of the brick making machine. Lambert B. Battin, the legal guardian of his father, brought suit to recover half of the profits, but the common pleas court of Lancaster County held that one joint owner of a patent cannot sue another for infringement or compel distribution of profits.

Despite all the years of litigation, Battin was not as poor as some people believed. With his inventive genius and business foresight, he resigned from the Northern Liberties Gas Company in 1845 to start a contracting business,

Battin, Dungan & Co. Battin was manager, and C. B. Dungan, who had worked with him at Northern Liberties, was secretary and treasurer of the new firm.

The company's first contract, with Battin in charge, was to construct gas works in Albany, New York. The capital of the Empire State found in Battin a clever engineer. He not only laid the main pipes and built a gas manufacturing plant way ahead of schedule, but he also improved the style of gas burners and invented a water seal valve to prevent the flow of gas while making repairs and improvements. "One of the most practical engineers that we have ever known," exclaimed H. L. Webb, president of the Albany Gaslight Company.

Battin's business skyrocketed. During the next four years he had contracts to build gas works in Newark and Paterson in New Jersey, New Haven and Hartford in Connecticut, Rochester and Syracuse in New York, Charleston, South Carolina, Richmond, Virginia, Reading and Scranton in Pennsylvania, and Washington, D. C. He did much of the work himself because he always considered himself a working man. Actually, however, it gave him a chance to better the gas equipment he installed.

In New Haven, for example, he conducted

a series of experiments with Benjamin Silliman, Jr., the noted Yale chemist, to show the advantage of coal gas over any other mode of obtaining artificial light. Spermaceti candles were rated second to coal gas at the time. They found that ten of Battin's batwing burners would produce as much light as 100 sperm candles. They found that it would cost the city about 22 cents an hour to make, from sperm candles, the same quantity of light as Battin's burners could give for two cents and four mills.

After constructing gas works in many large cities, he turned his attention to water works. His most notable engineering feat was the construction of a tunnel under Black Rock Harbor, in Niagara River, for the purpose of supplying the city of Buffalo with water from Lake Erie. It took almost two years to complete the job. After that — in 1852, to be exact — he dissolved the firm to devote more time in fighting those who tried to use his coal breaking machines without paying royalties.

With the advent of the Supreme Court victory, some citizens of Elizabeth, New Jersey, repeatedly asked him to construct a water works for the sprawling city fourteen miles southwest of New York City. Finally, he resisted no longer. They organized a water company and made him its first president. He liked the place so much that he moved his family from Newark, where they had lived for 22 years after leaving Philadelphia, to a large brownstone mansion, on South Broad Street in Elizabeth.

Few cities had seen any figure like this inventor, dressed in a black linen suit, a white shirt with a Spanish collar. His fiery eyes, deepset as the coal shafts into the side of a mountain, gave his Van Dyck-trimmed face a double-edged appearance, and it was heightened by a leonine head of flowing white hair. His mustaches gave no clue that he suffered from varicose veins, for they curled outward as if he were a man bursting with energy. And of course he was. He showed his inventions in public to complete the classic picture of an eccentric inventor.

One day when he was still president of the Elizabeth Water Company he appeared before City Council for a permit to use a steam carriage along the streets. The president of City Council looked at him as if he did not quite understand.

"Come out to see it," Battin urged.

The councilman were amazed. The steam engine was built in the form of a man and equipped with large wheels. Battin hid himself inside the curious looking vehicle and started the boiler. He set the car in motion and traveled down the street and back. Members of City Council nodded their heads. The steam man, as Battin was called from then on, received a permit to use it as a public vehicle.

He didn't consider himself too old to drive the heavy car wherever he pleased. Often he took it to the state fair at Waverly, near Elizabeth, and in between horse races he rode it around the fair ground track, amusing thousands of spectators. Because the vehicle weighed a lot, little bridges were constructed along the routes he usually took so that he could cross gutters without calling anyone for help. When too many horses reared in alarm at the contraption, Battin finally abandoned it. But some of the dents the steam carriage made in street curbs are still seen.

His contribution to the cause of free education is better remembered in Elizabeth today than anything else he has done. For the simple reason that on March 23, 1889, he turned over to the city the deed to his $250,000 mansion for purposes of a high school which now bears his name. Its interior was all of carved oak and mahogany, the grand winding staircase alone costing $40,000. In his letter with the deed Battin said:

"The experience and observation of my long

life have taught me that 'Knowledge is Power.' In making this gift it is my earnest wish and hope that every available means for education shall be afforded the youths of our city who may come after me."

The entire city came together to thank him for his gift. "Today," boasted the Elizabeth *Daily Journal* of March 26, 1889, "Elizabeth owns the most magnificent high school building in the state of New Jersey."

Meanwhile Reverend Albert Simpson, president of the Christian Alliance and pastor of Gospel Tabernacle in New York, saw in the venerable citizen of Elizabeth a financial angel for new temples. From then on "Simpson followed him closely, coddling him in every possible way, and endeavoring to wheedle money out of him." Though reared in the Quaker faith, Joseph Battin changed to the Baptist church upon his marriage, and in his later years gave liberally of his means toward the support of religious and charitable works. He had no dealings with doctors, and when he believed he was relieved of varicose veins by his faith in God, he became a convert to the faith cure doctrine.

After he gave the Christian Alliance a $100,00 building in New York and land in Elizabeth on which to build a faith cure temple, his children became alarmed lest the faith curists should get all his money. By that time, however, Battin had made ample provisions for his children, and refused to change his course. He was so infatuated with faith curism that he moved out of his daughter's home in Elizabeth to the Berachah Home, in New York, where Reverend Simpson lived. Four months later in August, 1891, two of his sons, Sylvester and Lambert, who stepped in to stop his remarkable liberality, were appointed his legal guardians.

Unlike Stephen Girard, who endowed Girard College for the education of orphan boys from Philadelphia and second from the anthracite region, the philanthropic Battin left no money for the education of coal miners' children. He left something else which forced young boys to leave school at the age of eight or nine in order to earn money picking slate in the breaker to help the family exchequer. There was no place more cruel and hopeless for a boy than a coal breaker. It not only left its mark upon the people of the coal belt, but also marked the area where man-made mountains of coal dirt, slate and rock were to rise somber and black toward the sky.

The coal breaker also left its mark upon the literature of the hard coal country. Russell Janney, for example, painted a lurid picture of a towering breaker to provide local color in the opening scenes of his novel, *The Miracle of the Bells*, which recently starred Valli, Fred Mac-Murray and Frank Sinatra on the screen. A little older in time, breaker boys are the heroes in Homer Greene's *Burnham Breaker* and Kirk Munroe's *Derrick Sterling*. Even Clarence Darrow, who visited the region with Johnny Mitchell, the miners' patron saint, during the anthracite strike of 1902, penned a short story called *The Breaker Boy.*

Since Joseph Battin's death on August 29, 1893, the coal breaker has changed a good deal in size and power. Today the breaker, as Janney writes, "could smile indulgently when cities boast of their skyscrapers." It now operates by electricity, each piece of machinery having a separate motor. Two of the largest coal breakers in the world, one at St. Nicholas and the other at Locust Summit, prepares at least 10,000 tons of coal daily for markets in New England and Middle Atlantic states. Despite all the modern improvements, Battin's idea of rollers and screens is just as much in vogue as the day he set up his first coal breaker near Minersville.

Chapter Fourteen

Father of American Minstrelsy

As 20-year-old Thomas D. Rice relaxed in the
dressing room of Ludlow's theater in Louisville,
Kentucky, one day in 1828, waiting his turn in
the rehearsal of *The Kentucky Rifle*, a three-act
play, he heard the plaintive notes of a Negro
folk tune coming from outside the window. He
stretched his elongated frame to gaze out. There,
in livery stable behind the town's legitimate
theater, was a Negro slave singing of his woes
as he cleaned and brushed a horse. His right
shoulder was drawn up high, his left leg was
stiff and crooked at the knee, and when he took
a few steps he limped ludicrously. At the end
of each stanza the shabbily dressed slave who,
as was the custom, assumed his master's name,
Jim Crow, shuffled his feet and rocked on his
heels as he sang:

> "Wheel about, turn about,
>   do just so,
> An' eb'ry time I wheel about
>   I jump Jim Crow."

Rice let out a mirthful laugh which echoed out on the stage where his tall, English-born director, Samuel Drake, was rehearsing other members of the traveling troupe. Drake rushed into the dressing room and saw the white actor leaning out the window.

"What the hell are you laughing at?" he yelled.

"Look at that stable hand," Rice pointed. "When he sings 'I jump Jim Crow,' he bends his body and kicks his feet like this."

"Come on, Rice," Drake said. "Stop the mimicry. Let's go on with the rehearsal."

But Rice did not stop. The youthful looking theatrical performer from New York took an interest in the Negro problem which was to divide the Nation, half-slave, half-free, and cause a great Civil War. Certainly this wasn't just a caricature if he took the time, between rehearsals, to observe the stable slave and to catch snatches of the Negro melody. Then in the dingy, cramped dressing room he practiced Jim Crow's peculiar dance and hummed the song until he quickened the rhythm. He asked Drake for permission to introduce the number between acts, but the black-haired theatrical manager said no. Rice waited until the premiere of *The Kentucky Rifle*, and when the first two acts of the play

254

failed to arouse the Louisville audience, he approached Drake again.

"Go ahead," Drake moaned, "it won't make any difference now."

In his regular costume, with burnt cork on his candy face, Rice appeared on the stage and swiveled his banjo eyes over the oil footlights. The audience of hard-scrabble farmers, rivermen and Southern gentlemen sat gloomily until he began to sing "Jim Crow," shuffling out an accompanying routine on the stage with his feet. The performance even made the new-sawn pine boards warp with laughter. He repeated it six times before the audience would let him go.

Rice's impersonation of Jim Crow laid the groundwork for the Negro minstrel show — a form of entertainment that many authorities consider the only distinctly American contribution to the theater. He started not only a flood of Negro melodies based on plantation life, but he also introduced the Negro style of dancing to the stage. The troubadours of the burn't cork circle who came after him added a great wealth of music to the new medium.

The name of Jim Crow had no special significance in Rice's early days. Today it has become synonymous with segregation. Negroes, in particular, abhor the influence of Jim Crow laws in Southern States where they are denied entrance to certain schools, restaurants, hotels, and other public places, and they therefore resented the type of Negro characterized by minstrels. Despite the present ramifications of Jim Crowism, the man who first sought out old Negro folksongs and imitated their peculiarities of manner, dress and speech on the stage is little known.

The father of black-faced comedians was delivered to an impoverished home in New York's Seventh Ward, now in the shadows of Manhattan Bridge, on May 20, 1808. The T. D. stood for Thomas Dartmouth, but many of his fellow showmen called him Daddy Rice. After receiving a common school education, he was apprenticed to Jeremiah Dodge, a wood carver who fashioned many figureheads for our early merchant vessels. But instead of holding wood in his hands he wanted some lighted boards on which to stand and perform in front of people. He abandoned wood carving.

In 1828, appearing as a supernumerary in *Bombastes Furioso*, a not-too-low comedy, at New York's Park Theater, he delighted in making fun on stage of the star performers, Tom Hilson and John Barnes. One day it excited the audience beyond measure. The two young English comedians were offended, and the applause thief, who was not even on the bill, was kicked out of the theater.

Leaving New York, he joined a group of itinerant theatrical performers called Ludlow's Players. Rice was its newest, youngest and skinniest member, and as such, he was fair bait for the extra task of stage carpenter, property man and lamp lighter. The company broke up in Mobile, Alabama, when a fire destroyed all the stage properties and forced Noah Miller Ludlow, a well-known theatrical manager of those days, out of business. Rice moved to Louisville and hooked up with Drake's company.

It was here that he lifted the Jim Crow characterization out of the theater alley. After the failure of *The Kentucky Rifle*, in which he ployed a corn field Negro, Rice found himself once more with Ludlow who, in 1829, began his second managerial effort in Louisville. This time the sprouting minstrel got a little better billing. In Cincinnati, where Ludlow rented the Columbia Street Theater for an entire season, Rice resumed his version of Jim Crow between acts.

Worried by the knowledge that he was no great shakes as a serious actor, Rice spent hours in front of mirrors practicing how to limn the Negro dialect, how to express their pathos and humor, and how to depict their foibles. Then he broke away from Ludlow's troupe and took a steamboat up the Ohio to Pittsburgh.

When he reached the Griffith Hotel in that city, he had an idea. The Negro who had carried his bags from the river landing to the hotel amused him as much as did the stable hand in Louisville, and their names were almost alike. This one was Jim Cuff. For a pastime he held his mouth open so that contestants on the streets could try to throw coins into it. The minstrel persuaded Cuff to go with him to the Fifth Street Theater where he had to put on a show. He borrowed the porter's pants, coarse straw hat, and shoes full of holes. The stripped Negro hid in the wings as Rice waddled into view of the Pittsburgh audience. The ill-fitting raiment produced an instant effect.

The black-faced singer opened his number with a short prelude of "Jim Crow," and shuffled his feet as though one leg were wrapped around the other like a dead twig. The uproarious laughter of the audience tickled more life into his singing of the chorus:

> I went down to de river
> I didn't mean to stay
> But dare I see so many gals
> I couldn't get away.

258

With each succeeding couplet the audience became more excited. A few minutes afterward Cuff heard the whistle of an approaching steamboat and realized that he had to get back to the boat dock. He tried to catch Rice's attention, but the freestyle minstrel was in a singing mood:

> I kneel to de buzzard,
> An' I bow to the crow,
> An' eb'ry time I weel about
> I jump jis so.

By this time the hotel porter sensed that his job was at stake. How soon would the song end? He could not wait. He stuck his head beyond the wing and whispered, "Massa Rice, Massa Rice, must have my clo'se! Massa Griffif want me — steamboat's coming!" But Rice sang of people in the audience and events that took place in Pittsburgh.

The porter whispered a little louder, but Rice seemed not to hear him above the din of applause. Finally Cuff cast all sense of propriety aside. He rushed toward the center of the stage, and just as the burnt cork artist, in his deep falsetto voice, was singing, "An' eb'ry time I weel about I jump Jim Crow," the Negro laid his bare hand upon the performer's shoulder.

"Massa Rice," he shouted against the uproar of the audience, "Ah wants mah clo'es. Massa Rice, gi me my nigga's hat, my nigga's coat, my nigga's pants — gi me my clo'es. STEAM-BOAT'S COMIN!"

The theater was in an uproar. The footlights were turned off. The curtain was lowered. Rice washed the burnt cork off his scapel-edged face and ran outside to a music store run by a young music teacher named William C. Peters. The minstrel asked his help to publish the song. The title page of the first edition, with Peters' pianoforte accompaniment, was decorated with a lithograph of Daddy Rice in his besmeared appearance. Within a few weeks after it was published, "Jim Crow" became the singing craze of clerks in the stores, ladies in the parlors, workmen in the shops and on the rivers, and boys in the streets.

The song spread all over the country. People in Philadelphia, Baltimore, New York and Boston waited eagerly for the appearance of the minstrel. His appearance was heralded days in advance, and many theaters were sold out before the first performance. Naturally Rice's success attracted imitators, but it is worth noting they played in groups. Rice performed alone.

In 1833, when he played in Washington,

D. C., he pulled a surprise. He walked onto the stage of the National Theater with a bulky bag slung over his shoulder and sang:

> Ladies and gentlemen, I'd have you to know
> That I've got a little darky here that jumps Jim Crow."

Turning the bag upside down, he dumped four-year-old Joseph Jefferson, who afterward became famous as an actor, before the eyes of the astonished audience. He was knee-high to the six-foot minstrel, and they looked like a pair who had just trooped in from a cotton field. They sang alternate stanzas of the Jim Crow song. It excited the theater-goers, and the miniature Jim Crow climaxed the performance by dancing.

Sought after for renditions of his song, Rice was always on the lookout for new material. When he reached a town, as he first did at Pittsburgh, he rubbed elbows with the people in the streets in an effort to humorize some of the events the citizenry were talking about in the chorus of "Jim Crow." And as he jostled with crowds in various localities, he learned more about the Negro problem.

Later on, he decided to offer his song with an olio — a mixture of dancing, songs and comedy sketches. For the most part, the olios reflected the hard times and good times, the poverty and pathos, the woes and triumphs of the Negro. Presently he composed Ethiopian operas to replace such performances.

One of the first of these — Virginny Cupids — was premiered at the Bowery Theater in New York when Rice was only twenty-four. Before shambling on the stage, he felt as tense as a piano string. Back and forth, he went up to the peephole in the curtain to count the house. As he sang his first ditty, Clare de Kitchen, he began to tremble at the knees. The song had practically a different idea in each verse and the audience seemed to be disappointed by its opening. Then Rice launched into a verse that mentioned Coal Black Rose, "She as black as ten of spades, and got a lubly flat nose." Nobody could hear his voice without knowing that he would burst with the emotions that trembled inside of him:

"Go away," says she, "wid your
    cowcumber shin
  If you come here again I stick you
    wid a pin;"
  So I turn on my heel and I bid her
    good bye.
  An' arter I was gone she began to cry.

As he reached the last verse, the tension in his body disappeared, and his voice radiated merriment as he stood on an enormous stage in front of a full house:

> I wish I was back in old Kentuck,
> For since I left it I had no luck.
> De gals so proud de won't eat mush
> An' when you go to court 'em dey say,
>   Oh Hush!

After that evening the one-act opera was better known as Oh Hush! than as Virginny Cupids. Clare de Kitchen was a radical departure from the love songs of Irish minstrels. Its plaintive air of suffering reflected the attitude of Negro slaves that singing was one sure way of loosening taut heartstrings. Next Rice sang "Gumbo Chaff," a ditty about a drunken Negro on the Ohio River. The minstrel ditties were so written that whoever sang them could make up his own verses to fit the tune and the occasion. With these numbers — not to mention "Jim Crow" — Rice drew more customers to the Bowery Theater than any other actor of his time. Some say that the old Negro melodies he put into his librettos built a wide public audience for the songs of Stephen C. Foster.

At once, he started to spend his income as freely as the sun which brightens every object on which it shines. He lived in the most luxurious hotels, where his boon companions were actors and writers who delighted in shocking social leaders. He wore buttons made of guineas, sovereigns, and gold pieces on buff or blue waistcoats with white cravats, sparkling with diamonds. People who never saw him before liked to sit and stare at him. He was a lean, rawboned man, with unruly dark hair. When he laughed everybody laughed with him, because it was the kind of laughter that made people feel good themselves. Some of his friends would lure him for a drink to some bar in order to listen to his stories and, in some cases, to rob him of his ornaments. Yet he would do anything to solace an aching heart.

One afternoon in 1834, in a Louisville hotel room, Junius B. Booth, a distinguished actor of tragic parts who suffered semi-lunatic attacks, asked him to get a human skull for use on the stage. Suddenly a clergyman, following Booth's request, came into Booth's suite. Rice followed them into the adjoining room where Booth lifted a black cloak off a small coffin in a table. The reverend jumped back with a look of astonishment and horror.

"Pray, sir, you requested me to come here and perform the funeral rites of the dead, and to my astonishment you present a poor pigeon."

"Well, sir," Booth remarked, "is it not dead?"

"Yes, but it is an animal."

"Well, sir, is not a man an animal?"

"Yes, but a pigeon is not a human being—it has no soul."

"How do you know it has no soul?"

"I won't be insulted," the minister answered as he moved toward the door, "and I hope your friend here will find a strait jacket for you as soon as possible."

The persons to whom Rice told this story ranged from Davy Crockett, early Southern humorist and folk hero, to Noah Ludlow, his former director, but the part he forgot to mention was that this by-play so delighted him that he got the head of a murderer who was hung for Booth. In return, the fiery, dissolute actor whose youngest son later assassinated President Lincoln played a blackface role in Rice's new Ethopian opera, "Bone Squash Diavolo." In this burlesque of Fra Diavolo, another theatrical success, Rice added "Such a Gettin' Upstairs" to his repertoire. It was an old river song, with no tinkling rhymes in it, but he had heard colored roustabouts sing it so many times that remembering it was easy.

On a Suskehannah raft I cum down de bay,

An' I danc'd an' I frolick'd an' I fiddled all
de way,
Such a gettin' upstairs I nebber did see,
Such a gettin' upstairs I nebber did see.

In 1836, the buoyant, wayward New Yorker
landed in England, singing "Jim Crow," and
soon had the big-wigs of London at his feet.
They formed a Jim Crow Club and got up at
their own expense lithographs of Daddy Rice.
He could make people laugh by hunching his body
or twisting his marshmallow lips. He went
through, first at the Adelphi and then at the
Pavilion, two shows a night. For several months
his success continued. He sang "Jim Crow" to
crowded houses in London, Edinburgh, Liver-
pool and Dublin. Before he was finished touring
the British Isles, he scored the first great hit
of an American song abroad and had rendered
it 1260 times, an exalted record that only a few
American performers have been able to surpass.
Negro minstrelsy became so popular there that
for the next fifty years American minstrel
troupes made extended tours abroad.

In the meantime he was fascinated by the
charm and grace of Charlotte B. Gladstone. She
was the daughter of his English manager who
first introduced Rice at the Surrey Theater. She
and Thomas were married on June 18, 1837, and

after a brief honeymoon in England, they came to the United States. They had four children—three girls and one boy, whom Rice trained to be an actor. The elder Rice was a changed man upon his return to old haunts. The black-faced comedian, exposed to British ways, quickly adopted popular cockney themes and discarded his more robust plantation topics. He did not, however, change over completely.

When he offered new Negro extravaganzas, the managers of all the major theaters in the United States sought his services. But not for long. Those who had first seen him in "Jim Crow" suddenly became puzzled by the change in his attitude towards the Negro and new impersonations. This wasn't the decrepit slave. This wasn't the slave who wanted his freedom. This wasn't the slave in the American scene and Rice obviously felt that the Negro problem was the same on one side of the Atlantic as on the other. But it wasn't. This was a Bond Street dandy with a chocolate complexion. His fans couldn't fathom it any more than an audience today would understand it if Jack Benny had suddenly thrust Arthur Treacher into Rochester's shoes. They were simply not interested in seeing Jim Crow as an English gentleman. After one good engagement — the reward of his earlier fame — Rice lost one lucrative offer after another until he found himself playing to a limited audience.

Although his farces of the dandy darky were not popular, the minstrel himself was still a favorite of many American theater managers. For his indulgence was something to remember. On one occasion Francis C. Wemyss, who managed a failing theater in Philadelphia, posted bills advertising "Jim Crow in London." In it Rice appeared as a bootblack at the court of St. James. The farce received a poor house, and when the time came to collect the sum specified in the contract, which was higher than the box office receipts, Rice said to Wemyss, "Lookye here, my master. This has been a bad job — I don't think you ought to suffer to this tune; live and let live is a good motto — hand over . . . , and I will give you a receipt in full, and wish you better luck another time."

With the growth of minstrel troupes, Rice found it harder to command packed houses. His "Jim Crow" seemed less popular, for several minstrel troupes were singing catchy Negro melodies that the public apparently enjoyed. The composer of them was Stephen C. Foster. As a small boy who grew up in Pittsburgh, Foster was often down on the river wharves, and many times he saw Rice when the father of American minstrelry used to debark from a steamboat and limp uptown to entertain theater-goers with renditions of "Jim Crow." Under the influence of the Jim Crow craze the young brown-eyed boy started to write songs of the colored people.

In the beginning he tried to sell some of them to Rice, but the fertile-minded minstrel turned them down because he still had enough rhymes to keep his own act going. It didn't matter to Rice whether they were good enough to compete with other songs. Didn't his name count for something? After several years in which his minstrel and plantation ditties lost some of their appeal, he came back with a Negro travesty of Othello. It squelched talk that Rice was washed up on the burnt cork stage.

In 1851, when Rice was forty-three and not as creative as in his younger days, Foster saw him again in Cincinnati. This time Rice purchased "Long Ago Day," an anti-slavery melody, for an undisclosed amount, and intended to use it in an Ethiopian opera. At the same time he showed Foster some verses for which he wanted him to write the music. It turned out to be "This Rose Will Remind You." His effort to use these songs in a new production were cut short when he suffered a stroke. He could use neither his voice nor his legs. Friends, whom he never lacked, held shows for his benefit until he was able to get back on his feet.

More than once in the course of the following years of poor health Rice thought he would live to produce a great anti-slavery opera. But he suffered from financial embarassment. He took on a succession of acting part in perennial favorites when he discovered that his paralysis took humor out of his performances of Jim Crow, and played with such minstrel troupes as Charley White's Serenaders and Wood's Minstrels. These were the few times he appeared in minstrel shows. He also played Uncle Tom in the dramatization of Harriet Beecher Stowe's great anti-slavery novel, but he hungered for a musical dealing with the same theme.

Every performance, however, affected his health. In September, 1861, after the outbreak of the Civil War, he suffered another stroke. This war was something terrible to him. The plaintive melody he had purchased from Foster came to his mind, and these words from "Long Ago Day" he rehearsed until his dying breath:

Long-ago day, down de lone way all my
    fren's has follow'd you
Ef de Lawd give me my own way, I'd surely
    follow'd too.

But I'se goin', soon I'se goin', soon I'll drop
    my trublin' load,
An' dere'll be more ob hoein' whar I'se goin'
    down de road.

Chapter Fifteen

Father of the American Navy

Joshua Humphreys, the Philadelphia shipbuilder who got a thrill out of designing the first
six ships of the U.S. Navy, is still fascinating
experts on American Revolutionary lore with the
quality of his ships. More than a century and a
half have passed since the buzzing of saws and
the banging of hammers were heard in his shipyard on the Delaware River, but only recently
proof of his unique workmanship popped up
again. On the New Jersey side of the Delaware,
opposite Philadelphia, some relic hunters found
hand-wrought nails, pieces of pewter, antique
metal buttons and other remains of a sunken
British man-of-war after being pumped through
a pipe line from the river bed.

As historians debated which of Humphreys'
ships sunk the foreign vessel, those who found
the relics decided to use part of the hardware in

the restoration of Pont Reading, a Colonial mansion near Ardmore, Pennsylvania, where Joshua Humphreys lived the last thirty-five years of his life. The sunken ship trove was enough not only to recall Humphreys' name but also to revive speculation of his proper place in history.

When he first tackled the models for the frigates in a Philadelphia mold loft in 1794, Humphreys had nearly thirty years of shipbuilding experience to fall back upon. He was born on June 17, 1751, in the present residential community of Haverford, Pennsylvania. His parents were Welsh Quakers. They moved to near-by Philadelphia, a thriving city with an important sea port, when Joshua was seven. After leaving school in 1765, he was indentured to James Penrose, an English-born shipwright, to learn the art of shipbuilding.

No sooner had he entered the small shipyard owned by James and Thomas Penrose than the young Quaker found himself in a hotbed of political agitation. The Penrose brothers, who would not import any goods from Great Britain so long as they had to pay duties into the English exchequer on articles imported from other countries, were in the forefront of the movement to repeal the Stamp Act. Through a crusading temperament they were able to inspire an almost doglike devotion to liberty in every member of their shipyard.

Outside the shipbuilding stocks the Penrose legend grew even more fabulous. For when the non-importation of raw materials threw Philadelphia artisans out of work, James Penrose, after his brother had cleaned out the great glue kettles, made soup out of salt meat, potatoes, beans, dry bread crumbs and doughballs. The unemployed artisans gathered daily in the Penrose shipyard. This was the first soup line in the country, and it is conceivable that young Humphreys took his turn in ladling out soup. If he had any mental conflicts because his Quaker religion forbade opposition to the British Crown, this humanitarian work during the Stamp Act riots took it right out of him. Ultimately he was read out of the Quaker meeting for giving aid to the Colonists against Great Britain.

Before he had completed his apprenticeship, however, James Penrose died and left the 20-year old apprentice to the whims of destiny. He served out his time as the widow-appointed executor for the vessels on the stocks and when he finished them Mrs. Penrose presented him with a beaver hat. Then, in 1772, he formed a partnership with his cousin, James Wharton. England still continued to press the thirteen colonies, and in the spring of 1774, when it closed the port of Boston, the Pennsylvanian Committee of Safety was concerned about the defense of its own sea port. It commissioned Humphreys and Wharton to build a gunboat, known as "Calevat," which carried two howitzers, swivets, muskets and pike. The vessel was also called a galley because it carried carlocks and oars like a regular galley. By the time the first Continental Congress met in Philadelphia the following September, the Committee of Safety had a Delaware flotilla of 13 gunboats, each manned by 53 men, and had the shipbuilders enlisted in the service of public defense.

Owing to the design and construction of the first gunboats, the qualifications of Joshua Humphreys stood out in the discussions of those who were appointed in Carpenter's Hall to handle naval affairs for the United Colonies. So he was assigned to the construction work in a Continental shipyard, and for the next five years worked under that Marine Committee. He designed the frigate Randolph, a swift sailing vessel with thirty-two guns, and fitted out the first fleet of the Continental Navy which left Philadelphia, in 1776, under the command of Captain Esek Hopkins. He worked day and night to keep the ships at sea. Then the man who made it possible for such heroes as Hopkins, John Paul

276

Jones and John Barry to carry the Rattlesnake flag with the motto, "Don't tread on me," on the high seas was almost broken-hearted when, after capturing 600 British vessels and achieving peace, the Continental fleet was scuttled.

The naval strength of the young republic had some resemblance to the naval situation of recent times. There were no warships to protect ocean-carrying trade. North African pirates came to take merchant ships at the mouth of the river approaches to Philadelphia, then the Nation's capital, and to crush American fortunes which, in the budding days of the republic, rested chiefly on the sea.

Humphreys went into the coffee houses around Independence Square to advocate the construction of a navy. As early as January 3, 1793, he wrote to Robert Morris, the senior senator from Pennsylvania, embodying his thoughts for the building of six frigates. He waited almost a year to see what Congress would do. The majority of legislators were not interested in a navy, and were hopelessly split into warring factions.

The Welsh shipbuilder was not daunted. He renewed his campaign with all the energy and fire in his well-knit, five-foot-eight-inch frame. Because there was no Secretary of the Navy in those days, he went to see Secretary of War

Henry Knox with his designs. George Washington eventually approved them, and Congress appropriated almost $700,000 to build six frigates. Without waiting for his appointment, Joshua Humphreys began his work as the first naval constructor in the United States.

He had no time to lose. For Congress provided that in case of amity with Algiers all work on the frigates would be stopped. The gray-eyed designer with whitewashed temples and heavy black eyebrows called for carpenters, joiners, coopers, mast makers, riggers, sail makers, chandlers and other workers. After building a mold loft, he prepared working plans for a 44-gun frigate, and while his assistants made copies of his master plan to supply to four shipyards, he drew the draft of two 36-gun frigates for additional yards.

To fight the privateers, Humphreys realized that he had to build each frigate capable of fast sailing qualities, steadiness of gun deck and heavier armament. He started work on the *United States* in his own shipyard, near Old Swedes Church, in Philadelphia, as soon as seasoned timber became available.

During the shaping of the infant navy, Humphreys performed a number of chores — drawing the drafts, making the molds, mustering all hands at the beginning and end of each work day and after returning from lunch, corresponding with the Secretary of War and shipbuilders, and revising his plans for the prefabrication of the vessels. He also supervised the laying of the keel on blocks, the bolting of the frames, the firing of the boiler to soak the white oak planks in salt water, and the spinning of yarns for the cables. He was the first person in any shipyard who ever directed putting up the frames of a ship from molds.

From the moment the keel was laid on blocks Humphreys, whose body looked like a long barrel on two piano legs with a thick mane of curly hair, was a familiar sight on the stocks. One day as he was about to raise bolted frames from the ground he heard the thud of horses. He looked up. Suddenly the handsome coach the horses were pulling stopped and out of it emerged a powerful built man with a pockmarked face. Humphreys' eyes popped. It was President Washington. The former surveyor from Virginia, in company with his grandson and Barry, came and engaged the naval construction in a discussion of the new naval designs. The idea of 44 cannons to a single deck created no little surprise. Years later Washington's grandson, George W. Park Custis, wrote that the chief executive was much gratified with "his first visit to an American Navy Yard."

In the meantime the Senate ratified a treaty of peace with Algiers and the work stopped upon the frigates. The Barbary states had hooked the United States on a pledge to pay $22,000 annual tribute and to give her a large quantity of naval stores. In the end the treaty cost us over a million dollars, and Washington didn't like it at all. He wanted to complete the nucleus of an American navy in an effort to stop this international blackmail. He never succeeded, for it was a presidential election year and the legislators were too absorbed in home politics.

Then, after election, they were anxious to see what would follow the inauguration of John Adams on March 4, 1797. Humphreys had confidence in Adams, for as a member of the Marine Committee appointed during the first Continental Congress Adams had acquired some knowledge of naval affairs. Presently Humphreys started a fire under the glue kettles in his shipyard and waited for word from the special session of Congress to go ahead on the frigate *United States*. As soon as the vote was taken, the not yet famous Stephen Decatur, then employed as a clerk in a Philadelphia counting house, ran to the shipyard with the order for Humphreys to resume. Bang! The yard sprang to work again.

To Joshua Humphreys, after sixteen months layoff, the smell of boiling glue, the tap-tap-tap of caulking hammers, the heave-hoing of sail makers testing the masts and the rolling of 24-Pounders into position was music to his ears. Two of his sons, Clement, 20, and Samuel, 18, who were learning the trade under him, shared his enthusiasm. So did the ship-carpenters, predominately Federalists, who were making the final touches to the frigate.

Not so Benjamin F. Bache, editor of the *Aurora*, a Democratic newspaper published in Philadelphia, who, in December, 1796, earned the wrath of Federalists for his editorial: "If ever a nation was debauched by a man, the American nation has been debauched by Washington." One day this scurrilous editor visited Humphreys' shipyard. The frigate was almost completed. Standing next to Humpheys' eldest son, Clement, Bache muttered, "What is Adams going to do with one forty-four gun ship? Send her to Africa to avenge the flogging given by an Englishman to the captain of an American ship?" There were a few words and then Clement attacked the editor. Bache preferred charges. "Yes, I am guilty," the 20-year-old Federalist said when taken before a magistrate. "I caned the the editor undoubtedly." So pleased were Federalists with his conduct that they paid the $50 fine and posted a $2,000 peace bond."

Except for Joshua Humphreys nobody waited for the launching of an American vessel as eagerly as the freemen who crowded the Delaware waterfront in Philadelphia on May 10. The frigate *United States* was the focal point of the naval debate and with her the present Navy was to begin. Starting at seven o'clock that morning Humphreys tallowed the launching-plank, took out the second tier of standing shores, and manned the capstans. Slowly the Delaware became jammed with flag-bedecked craft. President Adams and members of his cabinet were on board the U. S. brig *Sophia*. Then, as they waited for high tide, Humphreys ordered his men to knock back the blocks from the keel and side.

Suddenly Humphreys noticed the strain of the frigate on the spur shores. For fear that an accident might happen, he ran to tell the men topside to cut the lashings of the cables. Fortunately the man in charge on board beat him to it. The ship gained way and splashed into the Delaware without hogging shortly after one o'clock. She was the first vessel completed by the United States under the Constitution and the first of the six frigates authorized by Congress to hit the water. The 36-gun *Constellation* was launched at Baltimore on

September 7 and the 44-gun *Constitution* at Boston on October 21.

Less than half as big as a modern destroyer, the length of the *United States* was 175 feet, breadth of beam 44 feet and weight 1,576 tons. She was a formidable addition to the naval armament of the country, and the inward curving of the sides above and below the water line gave her the sharp lines of the Baltimore clippers to cut the water like a rapier. She carried enough sail to outdistance anything she met. She cost, Humphreys estimated, $27,000 less than either the *Constitution* or the *Constellation*.

After leaving her in the able hands of Captain Barry, Humphreys set up the blocks again to construct vessels, including a frigate, a brig and a schooner, for the Dey of Algiers. The neighboring pirates looked upon such tribute payments with envy and demanded equal treatment with the Dey. As the United States was in no mood to be pushed around, it prepared more vessels to enter the Mediterranean. Humphreys not only built some of these ships but he also built the frigate *Philadelphia* for his townfolk who presented it to the government, which now included the navy as a separate department.

Plans for most of the new ships passed over Humphreys' drawing board. He brought other shipyards into the business of building them. He also probably started the practice of subdividing contracts when he farmed out work to blacksmiths, tinsmiths, silversmiths and other artisans.

One of the most prominent artisans who believed in Humphreys and did work for him was Paul Revere. As only clues are available, it seems Humphreys, after meeting Revere on the first of his many rides in the City of Brotherly Love in 1774, kept in touch with the Boston silversmith and had him make copper bolts and spikes for the Navy's first frigates. Then, when the piratical nations of North Africa became more insolent, the government engaged Revere to roll sheet copper for a larger Navy. Humphreys furnished him with the copper ore and suggested ways of rolling copper for ship bottoms. All that we know of the rest of the story is that Revere, in a letter written to Humphreys on January 21, 1801, mentioned that he had smelted and refined the copper ore and asked Humphreys where he could get more of it.

It was also during this period that Adams resolved to do something more than just establish the Navy Department and put ships into the water before he went out of office. Hence on January 29, 1800, his Secretary of the Navy ordered Humphreys to examine several ports for the purpose of selecting the most suitable one for dockyards.

The 48-year-old naval architect left almost completed designs for some 74-gun ships on his table to survey the ports of New London, Newport, Boston, Portsmouth, Portland and Wicasset in Casco Bay. With the advent of the Jefferson administration, however, his port recommendations as well as his ship designs were laid aside. Building a strong navy was not in Jefferson's plans, and the economy axe swung down on Humphreys' head.

For a long while the designer of the infant navy felt lost. He could not go back to private shipbuilding, for all his old trade, now shifted to other yards, was afraid to move in the face of the Barbary marauders. Although the government thought of him now and then, as in 1806 when he he was commissioned to purchase land in Philadelphia for a Navy Yard and to lay out one in Washington, D. C., Humphreys lived in retirement at Pont Reading from 1803 to his death on January 18, 1838.

Even so, he did not forget his friends. Perhaps his longest friendship was with Thomas Truxton, who had gone to sea at the age of twelve, and the letters which passed between them expressed a warm appreciation of each other's gifts. In January, 1809, they met on a political level. With thousands of Federalists they marched to Independence Square to hold a meeting in protest to the embargo. Truxton presided. The meeting voted to form a committee to draw up resolutions against the embargo act to send to Congress, and Truxton appointed Humphreys to it.

When the time came to read the resolutions, hundreds of Democrats tried to disrupt the meeting. They beat drums, waved flags, and shouted like Indians to drown out the committee report. When the rioters finally tried to take over the platform, hundreds of sailors who had served under Truxton drove them off and outside the fringe of Federalists. Not until then were the resolutions read and passed.

Whereupon the sailors took the chairman's chair from the platform, put their adored Truxton into it, and carried him in triumph to a nearby coffee house. For want of a grip on the honored chair, the other sailors carried Humphreys and other members of the resolutions committee on their shoulders to the place of celebration.

Back in Pont Reading, Humphreys was justly proud of the officers and men who sailed in ships of his design through the glories of the undeclared war with France, the war with the Barbary States, and the War of 1812. His groundwork in building fast sailing warships with steadiness of gun deck and heavier armament helped make the Navy into what he believed it should be—a brilliant and mature expression of America's fighting power. His designs caused radical changes in the construction of warships of all nations.

Despite his achievements, he is an extremely underrated figure in American history. In the use of the title, Father of the American Navy, he always ran next to President John Adams and Commodore John Barry. Perhaps the reason he ranked third is that the scope of his work has never been understood. Yet if it were not for his naval designs which largely won friends and influenced legislation in the first place, the United States would not have had a navy until years after Adams had retired from the presidency and Barry was buried in a Philadelphia churchyard. The judgment and foresight of this self-educated naval architect and builder deserved vindication because two of the frigates built from his models —the *Constitution* and the *Constellation*—have survived the long stretch between our tiny, but tough, first navy and the atomic age.

Chapter Sixteen

Father of Patent Medicines

The credit, "Dyottville Glass Works," or "T. W. Dyott, M. D.," has appeared on countless bottles and flasks for over 100 years, yet the chances are that the name Thomas W. Dyott will leave you blank. Undoubtedly the people who creaked westward across the plains in covered wagons carried bottles of Dyott's medicine in their trunks just as city dwellers who could not afford a medical doctor kept some of his nostrums in their closets. People still treasure Dyott's glassware because he molded the face of early heroes like George Washington and the Marquis de Lafayette on the sides of flasks. He also thought enough of himself to mold his portrait on the opposite side of a flask with that of the esteemed Benjamin Franklin.

Few persons today have any idea of the swath Thomas W. Dyott cut in the life of America in the first half of the nineteenth century. More than any other man, he spread self-medication as far inland as settlers had gone and with the aid of newspaper advertising he sold remedies on a large scale. He was the first and largest wholesaler of balms, ointments, drops and pills in the United States, and hundreds of druggists, china merchants, and country storekeepers depended on him for their patent medicines and various sorts of bottles and vials. He even equipped apothecaries' shops with wicker baskets, chemical apparatus and glass cases in which to display patent medicines and sundries.

Today more than 1,000 manufacturers each year take about 365,000,000 dollars of the people's money through 58,000 drug stores in the United States for specially prepared packages of drugs and medicines. Like the modern drugstore, Dyott branched out in the field of education, banking, glassmaking and journalism and ended up with being one of America's first business entrepeneurs. As a result of his inroads an apothecary shop has now become a small department store where one may get not only drugs and prescriptions filled but also cosmetics, rubber goods, surgical supplies, toiletries, cigars and cigarettes, newspapers and magazines, novelties and lunches.

The patent medicine industry did not grow up overnight. It existed in one form or another as far back as anyone can remember, but it began to take its present shape in 1806 when Thomas W. Dyott, an immigrant of English and Scotch ancestry, painted "Patent Medicine Warehouse" on a shingle over his tiny drug store at 57 South Second Street, in Philadelphia. It was meagerly stocked with stomach elixir, stomach bitters, rheumatic drops, cough medicine, lozenges, laxative pills, itch ointment, corn plasters, and mineral water.

Dyott did not look like a man who could parlay this list of remedies into a huge trading business. Few men made as bad a first impression upon customers as he did. He was tall, stiff as a ramrod, with big, clumsy feet, and a cold, abstract face which Nathaniel Hawthorne might have had in mind when he wrote "The Great Stone Face." His customers felt that he was a walking icicle, for he wasn't much of a talker except when making a bargain. But even when he broke his silence, his English accent was as dull as the coarse texture and sober tints of his garments. Yet he rose in the drug world because he exploited the mails and newspaper to sell his nostrums.

No detailed knowledge of Dyott's early life has come down to us. The date of his birth is confusing. At the time of his death in 1861, some of the Philadelphia newspapers reported that he was ninety years old. His death certificate in the files of the City Hall states he was 84. Dyott himself, in 1839, when a judge asked him how old he was, said, "in my seventieth year," which would place his birth somewhere in England about 1770. He also said that he was the grandson of the celebrated Dr. Robertson of Edinburgh. This doctor probably furnished Dyott with some ancestral prescriptions, for in 1809, when he moved to 116 North Second Street, he advertised himself as "Proprietor of Robertson's Family Medicines."

Dyott first became interested in drugs in London, where he was a druggist's apprentice, and later in the West Indies. When he landed in Philadelphia in the middle of the 1700's, he did not have enough money to open an apothecary shop. He shelled out the few shillings in his pockets for a room not far from Independence Hall and tramped the streets in search of work. Along these streets came the greats of Congress and Colonial Philadelphia, and the way they neglected the appearance of their boots gave the quick-witted immigrant an idea. He concocted a liquid shoe-blacking and turned his room into a shoeshine parlor, and when he said, "Shine, mister?" the city's leading citizens put their feet on his stand. Some then took home a bottle of polish to keep up the pristine glory of their shoes.

By 1810 he saved enough money from America's first shoeshine parlor to go into the drug business. He added M.D. after his name, probably because he not only supplied drugs but also diagnosed the complaints of his customers, as did the apothecaries of England until 1866, and told them what medicine to use for treatment. The medical practice in the American colonies largely followed that of the mother country. If a physician tried enough drugs, the sick person was bound to get better, and apothecaries had nothing to lose by concocting drug cures for their customers. Instead of mixing drugs to combat a specific disease, Dyott mixed enough to loosen up the coughs and congestions of an entire regiment.

As the demand for his products grew, he moved to larger quarters, on the northeast corner of Second and Race streets, and turned a fast dollar wherever he could. He had a habit of buying and bantering for large quantities of such goods as yarn and oil lamps and selling them along with his patent medicines. When the demand was too heavy for his employees, he left his desk and packed bottles in separate packages, tying and labeling each one by hand, in order to keep up service. His signature as the sole proprietor, T. W. Dyott, M.D., appeared on the bottle labels and on the outside covers. He advertised his medicaments, priced from 25 cents for a box of pills to $2.00 for a bottle of stomach elixir, through newspapers in various parts of the country. With these medicines he sent, printed cheaply on a slip of paper, directions either in English, German, French or Spanish for their use.

With the advent of the War of 1812, the supply of bottles from England was cut off, and the few glass works in this country were not enough to meet the demand. The self-styled M.D. then decided to make his own glass. He had a previous experience to fall back upon, for when he sold shoe polish he needed special sizes of bottles which weren't imported. He walked to the Kensington Glass Works, three miles away, to have them made. He also served as an agent for two New Jersey glass works. He was so successful that in 1818 he took over a small bottle-glass furnace in Kensington.

Then new shapes of bottles began to form and glow in his mind. All kinds, big and little, white and olive and amber and aquamarine. He turned out an endless stream of odd perfume and toilet bottles, mustard jars and demijohns, apothecary vials and glass stoppers. In no way more did his artistic imagination show itself than in his pint flasks with their carved figure-heads of prominent patriots on the sides.

Slowly he realized that the intemperate and profane habits of his glass blowers stood in the way of his establishing the largest plant of its kind in the country. "I can't stand this terrific heat without taking a drink." an experienced glass blower told him when he tried to cut the use of spirits in his glass factory.

Then he conceived the idea of training boys with entirely different habits to take the places of old glass blowers, rosin pounders, batch makers, carters, and bottle grinders. He anticipated Girard College, the 100-year-old Philadelphia institution which teaches each of its students a trade, by twenty years.

The village he built on 400 acres of swampland on the Philadelphia side of the Delaware was as earth-shaking as the one Robert Owen, an English social reformer, laid out in New Harmony, Indiana, about the same time. Besides five glass furnaces, Dyottville consisted of forty brick dwellings for glass workers and apprentices, several maintenance shops, a wharf, sand washers and a boathouse. The surrounding farmland, under the supervision of Dr. Dyott's younger brother, Michael, provided all the foodstuff for the self-contained community.

Perhaps the 170 apprentices, who combined manual training with education, were the most interesting feature of Dyottville. Predominately orphans just as at Girard College later, they formed the keystone of Dyott's dream of a glass empire. He outlined a curriculum which called for them to spend the entire day in the glass factory. After supper, washed and dressed in fresh clothes, the boys went to s c h o o l on the grounds.

Sometimes Dyott rode out there for a get-together with his apprentices, but he didn't stay long. All lights in the village were turned off and the gates closed at 9:30 P.M. "No Alcohol Allowed" signs were posted in conspicuous places. The shaggy-haired glassmaker was attended by a lackey in a gold-braided livery and rode in a splendid English coach drawn by four horses.

He was not always o s t e n t a t i o u s with his money. His journeymen frequently had to sue him for back wages, which were at best from 12½ to 50 cents a day. The apprentices got only enough for pocket money. In 1833, when he realized the shortcomings of his glassmaking empire, he gave his workmen a chance to buy shares in Dyottville and establish it as a perpetual enterprise. He applied to the Pennsylvania legislature for an act of incorporation as a manufacturing and banking institution, but the glass manufacturers of other sections objected.

To meet his critics, Dyott engaged Stephen Simpson, an able journalist who believed as Robert Owen did that "all wealth is produced by labor." Soon afterwards, there appeared in the columns of the American *Centinel* (spelled with a "C") bold, defying, scathing attacks upon those who opposed Dyott's plan of perpetuity. "Jefferson," as Simpson signed the articles, ridiculed the charge of monopoly of Dyott's enemies and claimed they wanted to break up Dyott's factory in order to take over his markets. Despite the fact that petitions favored Dyott two to one, the Harrisburg lawmakers failed to grant him a charter.

Despite this defeat, Dyott continued his usual chores — thinking up new glassmaking ideas, preparing drug mixtures, checking the departure of Conestoga wagons with his nostrums for outlets in Baltimore, Pittsburgh and other large cities, and handling the other details that established him as the largest bottle and patent medicine man in the United States.

He was not satisfied with this business alone. After President Andrew Jackson crushed the Bank of the United States, Dyott opened the Manual Labor Bank on the same corner as his drug business. The general suspension of specie payments enabled him to throw into circulation thousands of dollars of his own notes in small denominations. Moreover, he started to pay his workers with these shinplasters drawn on the Manual Labor Bank.

These notes bore a handsomely engraved picture of a glasshouse interior flanked on one side with a portrait of Benjamin Franklin and on the other with one of Dyott. The engraver apparently used an oil painting by John Neagle for a likeness of the worthy doctor.

Neagle's portrait provided a realistic picture of Dyott at the height of his fame. The Philadelphia artist had his full share of famous sitters, but never one like Dyott. Robust and thick-set, his face surprisingly alike Lafayette, Dyott sat in repose, his head turned three-quarters to the left. The face with ruddy cheeks, Grecian nose and a small, proud mouth was deeply indented with the lines of thought, typical of men who like to think and speculate rather than to talk, and his deep-set eyes were filled with the lustre of unalterable determination. He was a bespectacled man with a cleft in his chin, flowing white hair, and a touching droop to the shoulders as if to heighten the effect of a flowing Windsor tie.

Although Dyott was worth only 700,000 dollars in real estate and medicine bottles, the portrait befitted a multi-millionaire. If Dyott thought he was rich, he was quickly disillusioned. No sooner had he opened his bank on February 2, 1836, than he ran into financial trouble. In order to stay in banking, he mortgaged his drug house and issued more notes. Three runs, one in February, another in March, and the third in April of 1837, stripped him of all his loose cash, saddled him down with more mortgages, and he vowed that he would never leave himself open again to such runs. Despite protests from his diminutive cashier, Stephen Simpson, who countersigned all notes, Dyott issued more notes than the value of his holdings.

The instability of the banking venture naturally took Dyott away from the patent medicine business for hours at a time. He was in the bank one day when he heard the creak of axles of a coach approaching slowly over the uneven cobbles of Race Street. The coach stopped in front of the bank and a well-groomed man got out. Dyott recognized him immediately as an agent from a neighboring bank and scrambled out the back way. The agent waited two hours to redeem $200 worth of notes. He refused to leave without the money. The cashier searched high and low and finally found Dyott in the drug house.

"Let him wait two more hours," Dyott replied.

When the financial conditions of the country did not improve, the practice of dodging his creditors grew too much for the aged entrepeneur. He started to unload his properties. Presumably he sold $150,000 worth of patent medicine, glassware, etc., to his son and nephew, John B. and Charles W. Dyott. He leased the glass works to his brother. He sold his furniture to his sister-in-law. Perhaps the only thing he did not give away was money.

About that time rumors rained upon the Cradle of American Drugs. One day it was this bank, the next day another bank that went under. Early on the first of November in the year of the financial panic creditors started toward the Manual Labor Bank. Dyott knew what was up. The creditors, hearing another rumor, were about to withdraw their savings. His teller knew what to do. The news spread like wild fire to the Dyottville glass factory, and soon men with glass dust in their hair, alone and in pairs, merged with those who wanted their money. As one of the Dyottvillers stepped up to the counter with a parcel of notes and asked for larger denominations, the teller miscounted the notes two and three times and finally sent the man away. Then another glass worker stepped up to the teller's window to exchange small notes for larger ones. The scheme to inspire confidence in the bank kept up all day. After the doors were closed, Dyott danced about in great glee. He had forestalled financial ruin. He took off his hat and spun it around like a top, as he frequently did, to show his extreme joy.

When more creditors reached the teller's window the next day, they invariably found someone in front of them with a parcel wrapped in silk cloth and saying "I want larger notes for these." The men then took the larger notes to Dr. Dyott in the drug store, two doors away, and later in the day took another package of small notes to the bank.

On the third day the white-haired banker was prepared to face angry creditors. He had mobilized a garrison of stalwart glass blowers and, armed with bludgeons, placed them inside and outside the bank. Men, women and children packed the high points that looked down upon the shrouds and masts of ships in the Delaware. They were excited but quiet with the foreboding of something evil to happen.

Then the calm broke. Dyott himself appeared on the front steps and held up his hands for silence. "Gentlemen," he cried, "you need not be all uneasy. I have enough to pay you all—if not in money—I have in goods."

But the crowd was not satisfied. It pressed closer to the steps and Dyott hastened inside the bank. One of the creditors, an Irish immigrant named Mike M'Grath, pushed his way as far as the big china knob of the door. "For God's sake," he yelled, "give me enough to get my kids out of Ireland."

"If you want to do that," Dyott replied, "use your credit to stock up with my medicine and open an apothecary shop."

After that the stores held by Dyott's relatives did an immense business taking in Manual Labor notes for merchandise. And what a variety! Of the two stores adjoining the bank, one offered Dyott's patent medicines and glassware and the other cloth, hats, boots, and suits. Not far away, standing like an outmoded apothecary shop, was a grocery store kept by Dyott's 16-year-old namesake. For more than a year this bartering system went on and drays and carts were busy hauling glassware from Dyottville so that Dyott could fill them with medicine.

Then all of a sudden Dyott announced bankruptcy. The windows of the Manual Labor Bank were boarded up, a sheriff's bill was nailed on Dyott's house and village, and the doctor applied for the benefit of the insolvent laws. The state, however, preferred charges against him for fraudulent insolvency. He was brought to trial on eleven counts. The mainstay of the prosecution was Stephen Simpson, and as a result Dyott was convicted and sent to Eastern Penitentiary for three years.

In prison his early efforts to save money with which to become a patent medicine man began to tell. He walked so much to skimp that now he had trouble with his legs and had to rub them with liniment. As a result of his condition he was pardoned before he served out his sentence, and returned to his old neighborhood to continue peddling his nostrums with his sons.

Although Dyott did not accomplish anything more until his death on January 17, 1861, he was as much a part of expanding America as the railroads which laced the country from coast to coast and border to border. Unquestionably many a sober, businesslike and respectable drug house today owes a great deal to the British immigrant who bottled his own medicine and taught more people self-medication than any other man before his time. The self-made doctor is forgotten today, but he exerted a tremendous influence.

Chapter Seventeen

Father of Farmers' Fairs

If a picture is worth a thousand words, a farmers' fair is a bird's-eye view of a thousand farms at a time. It is the biggest drawing card the farmers have to show new breeds of live stock and the new varieties of fruit, grain and vegetables. More than 2,000 agricultural fairs in the United States and Canada attract as many persons as live in New York, New Jersey, Pennsylvania, Ohio, Indiana, Illinois and Michigan. No institution has done more to help the farmer with his problems than the agricultural fair, yet Elkanah Watson, a many-sided man who first made it as important in the farmers' calendar as Christmas and the Fourth of July, is now hardly ever mentioned.

In 1807, when he abandoned a banking career to become a farmer, Elkanah Watson realized the last of his great ambitions. For twenty years, during which he traded across the ocean, cham-

pioned inland waterways, free schools, and turn-
pike roads, and organized the first bank at the
gateway to the West, he held a fierce and unquenchable love for farm life. Scarcely did he
know how much he was to change the pattern
of farm life in the United States in the next
century.

Upon moving to a large farm near Pittsfield,
Massachusetts, he was shocked to learn that
American imports of foreign woolens were cut
almost in half on account of the Napeolonic wars.
Dozens of woolen factories were threatened with
disaster. Watson, who had always encouraged
home-grown products anyway, decided at once to
promote the breeding of fine-wooled sheep in order to provide suitable raw materials for the
Berkshire woolen mills. He secured from Robert
Livingston, a diplomat who had imported Merino
sheep from France some years earlier, a pair of
pure-bred Merinos and began raising them on his
farm.

The Berkshire farmers were not taking the
wool shortage as he was. To awaken their interest, the ex-Albany banker showed his two Merino
sheep in Pittsfield's elm-lined public square. The
farmers came to see them and were quick to realize
the sheep had finer wool than their own native
sheep. They couldn't get over it. Watson watched

them with interest. "If two animals are capable of exciting so much attention," he asked himself, "what would be the effect on a larger scale, with larger animals?"

His curiosity was aroused. It gave him the idea of holding an annual cattle show and inviting farmers to show the public their prime animals. He accepted the challenge when he was fifty, began riding from farm to farm, and doubtless would have put on a spectacular show if the farmers had paid more attention to their animals. Most of the animals he saw were too poor to exhibit. He talked to everyone he met about raising Merino sheep and paying more attention to their livestock. In addition, he set an example by stocking his farm with a pair of small-boned, short-legged, grass-fed pigs and a prize English bull. His enthusiasm flowed over into the activities of his family.

No one who paid a visit to the Watsons shortly after Elkanah Watson had taken up farming forgot the picture of the happy menage at that time. Rachel Watson, whom the enterprising merchant married in 1789, made a good country wife and laid aside the city airs as effortlessly as a schoolboy taking off his coat. Their oldest daughter, Emily, then 17, sang in response to the robins or went with Mary, her 11-year-old sister,

307

to weed the flowers in the garden. George, two years younger than Emily, enjoyed feeding the ducks in the pond on the estate, and Charles, not quite ten, found it more amusing to go after butterflies with five-year-old Winslow close on his heels.

The individual pursuits of the family stopped, the noise died away, the moment the champion of fine-wooled sheep stood before them, a stocky figure in a flowered lapeled waistcoat, a square face with a Puritan jaw, a man who commanded the attention of his family whenever he was home.

Watson did not in the least physically look like a New England farmer. Quite the opposite: he was a flashy, finger-snapping man with unfathomable brown eyes and a chest which indicated he was a man of gargantuan appetites. A bickering, wrangling, sneering, pistol-packing papa of the frontier days, he had a prophet's conviction about anything he set out to do.

In the field of promotion he had no peer. He spent a good part of his lifetime proving that he could get things done. As a leader he had only one weakness, nobody could tell when he would pull out of a venture; by dint of this idiosyncrasy he kept his generation occupied with a host of projects.

His resemblance to the New England farmer

began and ended with his agricultural duties. His character was compounded of equal parts of dreamer and promoter, a happy combination which made it possible for him to drive ahead on a project without losing confidence in himself. He had a radical turn of mind; he liked to take feudal practices and change them to fit a democratic republic, as he had proved in Albany by fighting the Dutch law which required an individual to own property before he could vote.

Shortly after settling down in Albany, the cellar of his home filled up with water which came in from the street and he asked the village council to repair the streets. He blamed the condition not only on broken pavements but also on the practice of draining water from the roofs of the homes upon the streets through long spouts. He shouted so much for road improvements that one day he was met by a group of Dutch housewives, waving grooms and yelling, "Here comes that infernal paving Yankee."

Born of Pilgrim stock at Plymouth, Massachusetts, in 1758, Elkanah Watson was bound to John Brown, prosperous merchant of Providence, Rhode Island, by his parents when he was fifteen. Soon afterwards he enrolled in Colonel Nightingale's cadet company and drilled on the Providence streets in a scarlet coat with yellow facings.

When the war broke out in April, 1775, he asked his employer to release him from the indenture so that he might go to fight in the patriot cause. Brown refused.

For a few months the indentured boy felt melancholic. Then Brown sent him to deliver one and a half tons of gunpowder to Washington's almost powderless forces at Cambridge. Watson was thrilled to meet the greatest figure in the land who, at the moment, was telling a militia colonel what to do with his men. Then Washington directed a young officer to go with Watson and show him where to store the powder.

After he became twenty-one Watson settled down to the business of making a living. He received an assignment from Brown to carry money and dispatches to Benjamin Franklin, who was then in France to represent the American cause, and on the way back the resilient Puritan from Providence saw an opportunity to open his own shipping business in Nantes, a lively port on the Loire River. No sooner had he entered into a partnership with a Monsieur Cossoul than he contacted a bronchial ailment and sought a change of air. He left his partner in charge of the business and spent a year at Ancinis in the study of the French language and customs and then traveled in France, Belgium, the Netherlands and

England. The depression of 1783 wiped out his business and he returned home without any of the 40,000 guineas that the business earned in the previous three years.

On this side of the Atlantic he managed to go into business again. Cossoul, with whom he continued to correspond, became his partner for the second time, and went to Port-au-Prince, Haiti, to handle the orders Watson sent him from Edenton, North Carolina. In 1786, when the West Indian trade was too slim to hold the partnership together, Watson left his properties sunk in mortgages, moved north and, after a study of the business opportunities of the water-level route to the West, settled in Albany, New York, in 1789. By virtue of his travels in the Netherlands, which he described in his "Tour of Holland," he filled himself with schemes to improve the inland waterways of the United States. He found a fertile field in York State for his schemes.

When the fascination of canals abated and other men came in to follow through on his ideas, Watson turned his attention to agriculture. The first product to attract his eye was maple sugar. It was not as good as he thought it should be, and he called upon the New York legislature to set up a fund to improve the quality of the sugar. But in 1807 his zeal for animal husbandry led him to

Pittsfield where he originated the Berkshire Cattle Show.

Some of the neighboring farmers did not share his enthusiasm for an exhibition. Watson traveled the farm belt. By the fall of 1810 he had convinced twenty-six of his neighbors to sign an appeal to the public. The day the Berkshire Cattle Show was scheduled, the public square was filled with people, noisy with the hum of conversation, the barking of dogs in the streets, and the banging of horses' hoofs, when Watson appeared with his choice livestock. Other farmers marched behind him. As the procession passed down the street, Watson broke his stride and stepped in front of the crowd. He called for three cheers. Thunders of applause swept the square. The farmers were thrilled. The exhibition was a success.

Watson, however, dreamed of bigger things. His next job was to organize a society of farmers for the promotion of the annual cattle show. He wrote to Elbridge Gerry, then governor of Massachusetts, and members of the state legislature for help in promoting agricultural improvements, and in return received a charter for the Berkshire Agricultural Society which put his brainchild on a lasting foundation.

The efforts of the Berkshire Agricultural Society made the second annual cattle show even more popular than the first one. It raised $70 to give away in prizes to the exhibitors of the finest livestock. Farmers vied with one another to win the prizes. The society's first president, Watson himself, also prepared an address to inspire the farmers to greater heights.

The event which drew the most attention was the parade. Four marshalls, mounted on gray horses, headed a half-mile procession of mechanics, flag-bearers, bands, stage coaches, marchers and animals. The stage-coaches, each portraying some form of domestic manufacturing, were not as colorful as the floats you see in parades today, but they helped to show the people in the post-Revolutionary period one way to escape foreign commercial dominance.

More colorful than anything else in the parade were the members of the Berkshire Agricultural Society. Watson dug down in his own pocket to buy two hundred cockades and adorned each one with two heads of wheat for members and three heads for officers. Many who saw Watson at the head of the marchers, dressed in his green-ribboned sprigs of wheat, high hat, and medals, applauded because he was such a beautiful sight to behold. The oldest member of the society, similarly dressed, held a plow drawn by sixty oxen.

The strongest and most consistent drive be-

313

hind Elkanah Watson was his superior showmanship. He was a showman of infinite resourcefulness. To the end of his days he tried to improve and popularize every product with which he was connected, including even the Berkshire exhibitions. In 1812, preceding the annual address and public announcement of prizes, Watson introduced a local minister to give a pastoral prayer. The year after that Watson arranged a grand agricultural ball to close the exhibition.

On his first opportunity to have women participate in the fair, as recipients of fifteen prizes in women's domestic manufactures in 1813, he suffered almost loss of face. He held a special exhibition of clothing products made by women, but none of the candidates showed up to claim several premiums of silver plate. For a moment he was frantic. Then the fertile-minded promoter thought of something. He went home for his wife, escorted her to the exhibition house, and sent messengers to tell the farmers' wives and daughters that she wanted to see them.

Within an hour the women of the village started pouring into hall where the cloth show was held. "This was one of the most grateful moments of my life," Watson wrote in his memoirs. "I immediately arose in the rear of the table, on which the glittering premiums were displayed, and delivered a formal address." After that he announced the names of the prize winners in the women's division.

Watson's efforts to keep the Berkshire Cattle Show going were not exactly easy. Although the Massachusetts legislature had given him a charter, it would not listen to any application for state aid to improve the wretched system of husbandry. Yet, in his way, the father of the agricultural fair managed to obtain funds with which to reward farmers who raised more and better crops and fatter livesock. One year his society awarded $400 in prizes.

About the same time Watson appointed several prominent farmers to travel through Berkshire county, in July, when the fields were in full bloom, and to select the entrants with the best standing crops for awards. Nothing made him prouder. He said, "To see a group of the most respectable farmers (as if under the solemnity of an oath), personally inspecting in their midst, fields of grain, grass, vegetables, etc., and also the state of the orchards, buildings, fence and farming utensils; and to witness the anxious candidate for premiums, attentively hearing every lisp favorable to his husbandry or probable success, is more exhilarating to the pride of patriotism than to view the gorgeous pageantry of palaces and their pampered tenants decorated in gold."

Whenever a public figure turned him down because his plan sounded too undignified, Watson found some way of getting his help. Once he wrote to John Adams, at that time president of the Massachusetts Society for Promoting Agriculture, for a share of its unused premium fund to advance agriculture. He was turned down. Before he could present his appeal in person, Adams replied, "You will get no aid from Boston. Commerce, literature, science, theology, are against you—nay, medicine, history and universal politics might be added."

Four years later, in 1816, when he was packing his household furniture to leave Pittsfield, Watson happened to learn that the old Massachusetts society had decided to hold an exhibition and cattle show. "What is the reason of this?" Watson asked the former president of the United States. Adams replied that his curt remarks had been influenced by the belief that his society should institute public exhibitions of its own.

The Massachusetts Agricultural Society was not the first organization to copy the Berkshire plan. Soon after Watson had firmly established the agricultural fair, the founders of the old agricultural societies, predominately gentlemen farmers, began holding annual exhibitions in order to bring the farmers together and exchange information. In that way the farmers were led to act for their mutual welfare and to take pride in their calling.

The success of the Berkshire Agricultural Society encouraged Watson to devote more and more time to the fair movement. In 1816 he resigned as president of the organization to become, as Judge Richard Peters described him, "an itinerant missionary gathering your own congregation." He went on self-arranged visits to establish agricultural societies upon the Berkshire model in rural counties. He went into farming areas uninvited; often he lectured to a handful of farmers in a cold, empty barn. But nothing discouraged him. No man ever walked the earth with a brighter idea of what he could do for the farmers.

Upon his return to New York the first society he organized was in Otsego County in 1817. In succeeding months he organized societies in Oneida, Schoharie, Montgomery, Rensselaer, New York and other counties, attended their fairs, and was the principal speaker at each one.

The vast and expanding list of agricultural societies in New York attracted the attention of Governor George Clinton, and at the right moment Watson asked him for state patronage to carry on the work of the agricultural societies and for a state board of agriculture to coordinate their activities. When the legislature received Clinton's request in 1818, Watson stirred a trifle uneasily. He was afraid the economy-minded members would kill the proposal as they did in Massachusetts seven years earlier. Scarcely had he rounded up a few friendly legislators to tell them how much the state aid would mean to the farmers than he was accused of selfishness and lust for office. Nevertheless, the New York body granted $10,000 for the farmers' organizations and dropped the other suggestion.

After that things happened too fast for Watson to ask himself if he aspired to office. In the absence of a state board of agriculture he tried to serve as a one-man board himself. In addition to writing letters and sending pamphlets to every prominent agriculturist in the county, the agricultural missionary wrote to American diplomats in various countries, asking them to aid in the introduction of improved animals, seeds and implements.

As a result he received many varieties of foreign seeds. Like Johnny Appleseed, he planted them in various places and in time saw them become predominant staples in their districts.

Dr. Samuel L. Mitchell, to whom Watson gave a specimen of wheat sent him from Spain, played a joke on the "Grand Agricola" without his knowledge. It was at a reception in the Mayor's office at Albany. Since Robert Livingston had passed away, Mitchell said to Watson that the weathen crown which the protagonist of sheep-shearing contests had worn, devolved on him. Simultaneously the eccentric farmer raised his hands over Watson's head and imagined he was crowning his temples with the wreath of Ceres. From the way he was sitting the seed planter could not see the ceremony taking place. The ladies who were present caught on to it and smiled to themselves. From that day on they called Watson the "Grand Agricola."

Watson probably reached the height of his success in the 1830's when the societies in New York gathered together to hold a state fair. By his letter writing and propagandist activities he stimulated the organization of more than 700 agricultural societies in the United States. Nearly every state, and for that matter nearly every county, had an agricultural society.

Most men in their middle seventies would have been content to rest on their laurels. But not Watson. Though he had built himself a large stone house at Port Kent, on the shores of Lake

Champlain, his spirit was always on the wing. In 1837, at the age of 79, he delivered his valedictory address before the Berkshire Agricultural Society. In between his numerous travels he tried to write an autobiography of his crowded life. But he never finished it. He died when he was 84 years old.

Watson succeeded in spreading his societies where others failed because he relied on the agricultural fair to enlist the interest of the working farmers. The plowing match had been a time-honored feature of many fairs since Watson's day, and when, after 1830, other agricultural implements began to be developed, the same principles were followed in testing and demonstrating at field trials and fairs. The fairs also permitted the breeders of livestock and the manufacturers of implements to reach a new group of buyers.

Today most fairs are no longer principally dependent upon educational features. Since Watson's death, many fair associations have added amusements like shooting galleries, ferris wheels, and horse racing. Spielers try to outdo one another with gaudy claims for the wonders of their shows. The county fair has certainly changed a lot, butit still has Watson's time-treasured judging of livestock and farm products, the machinery demonstrations and contests, and the

the address of some prominent figure.

Elkanah Watson left a broad mark on his age, and deserves to be remembered as much today as he was when he was an agricultural missionary. He always did what he could to uplift whatever part of America came within his influence.

Chapter Eighteen

Father of Book Reviewers

Late in April of 1849 George Ripley, a pale, slender man with brown curly hair, cold, piercing black eyes, and the air of a philosophical Puritan preacher, entered the *Tribune* building at the corner of Spruce and Nassau Streets, New York, and noted a young man, sitting in front of his office door, who looked as though he was waiting for him. Ripley was editor of *The Harbinger*, leading weekly newspaper of Fourierism in the United States, and was now returning to his office after a lengthy illness. Before he walked into the deserted office, the youth handed him a note. The editor of *The Harbinger* read the note and found himself at once strangely drawn to the office of Horace Greeley in the same building.

The editor of the New York *Tribune* was seated at his old, high desk in the midst of correspondence and galley proofs. Laying his pen on the ponderous inkstand, his face fairly glowed with pleasure as he greeted Ripley in a thin, husky voice. He had met this champion of Fourierism when he was a frustrated clergyman milking

cows and teaching arithmetic at Brook Farm, a
self-sustaining colony on the outskirts of Boston.

He had called Ripley to tell him what had happened to the Fourierist weekly during his
absence. It lacked funds to keep in existence.
Slowly he changed the conversation to his own
newspaper, the principles that led him to start it
in 1841, and the members of his staff whom they
both knew from their work in social reform. He
had hardly finished telling him that Margaret
Fuller, a fractious woman who refused to devote
her space in the *Tribune* always to literature, had
gone to Italy to live when he was seized with an
idea.

From behind his narrow spectacles he observed his visitor. In his weak, querulous voice
he asked, "Would you like to have her job as
literary critic?"

Ripley looked at Greeley across the desk without a change of expression. "Literary critic," he
repeated, and sat there a moment in self-enforced
silence. The *Tribune* reached a wider public than
The Harbinger. It would be interesting, Ripley
thought, to review the books he read in such a
newspaper. Instead of a few hundred readers he
would have thousands of readers. "Yes," he finally said, "I think I'd like it!"

Literary criticism was, of course, nothing new

to him. In Greenfield, Massachusetts, where he was born October 3, 1802, he grew up in an atmosphere of books. He was the ninth of ten children, and since his little brother William died at the age of four, he remained the youngest of the family. His father, who was more interested in law books and politics than in business, served in the Massachusetts legislature when he entered Harvard at the age of sixteen, where he made his mark as a brilliant student in languages and literature. He was the top man of his class, and proceeded with the study of theology as a matter of course. With the eminent Dr. William Ellery Channing as his mentor, he easily learned the fine points in the writings of Socinas and Servetus and displayed an intellectual vigor that promised a successful career. In 1826 he was ordained into the Unitarian society and put in charge of a new church in Boston's waterfront district.

Immediately he set out to drop seeds of Christian truth wherever he found a listener. His excellent command of English had won him a number of friends, and they encouraged him to write for the religious periodicals. Afterwards he became editor of the *Christian Register*, which, in his hands, was as strong as his sermons from the pulpit. To serve the pulpit he had to keep up

325

with Unitarian thinking; to write about the views
of religious leaders he had to read their books.
He imported the latest books in German philosophy and criticism.

All of a sudden he realized that Friedrich
Schleirmacher, Johann Herder and other Pro-
testant clergymen had begun to reconcile scientific and philosophic truths with true religion
and Christian theology. In 1832, shortly after the
death of Johann Pestalozzi, a Swiss educational
reformer, Ripley called upon Unitarians to apply
new methods to their problems. That he should
accept the liberal teachings of Schieirmacher and
Pestalozzi was not pleasant to the mind of An-
drews Norton, a Biblical scholar who believed
that spiritual knowledge came by special grace
from God.

As the teachings of the Transcendentalists
gained followers, the former Harvard professor
of sacred literature attacked the new philosophy.
In 1837, after reading Ripley's review of Mar-
tineau's "Rationale of Religious Inquiry" in the
Christian Examiner, Norton called the sober
devoted minister of the gospel an "infidel." Although he denied the charge, Ripley realized that
he could not speak out on all subjects which were
uppermost in his mind without incurring the
charge of heresy. As a man of principle he could

not practice a doctrine he disdained. In 1841, one of the strongest pulpit-speakers in Boston who, for nearly fifteen years, preached Unitarianism, left the ministry.

Now fully aroused to the abuses, cruelties, and iniquities of the social order, the earnest man of thirty-nine advocated an enterprise of associated mind and labor. Sophia Willard Dana, daughter of a Revolutionary patriot whom he married in 1827, was equally sympathetic with his viewpoint. "Mrs. Ripley," Theodore Parker observed in his journal, "gave me a tacit rebuke for not shrieking at wrongs, and spoke of the danger of losing our humanity in abstractions." Pooling their life savings, they bought a 200-acre milk farm from which the colony took its name and, with Ripley's sister and fifteen others, took possession of the farm house. Lack of money narrowed the Brook Farm enterprise and kept its income at a low level. The group thought it had a chance of growing by embracing Fourierists in its cause, but the conversion of Brook Farm into a modified Fourierist Phalanx in 1844 proved its ruin.

As things turned out, it was one of Ripley's most propitious mistakes. It knocked him out of utopia and into a job on the New York *Tribune*. It eventually gave him a name, money, and an opportunity to start something new in American life.

New York, the city of his greatest success, was a place of bitter suffering during his first years. He lived in a small room; he could afford no better quarters for himself and his wife. Two years before and after he moved to New York he edited *The Harbinger*, and the small pay he received for this work was spent as soon as it was received for food and shelter.

He didn't mind the privations. He said he would pay off all the debts of Brook Farm, and even to reimbursing the stockholders like Nathaniel Hawthorne. He sold his library of fine books to pay off some creditors. Still, his debts exceeded $1,000. His wife tried to help him. She obtained a teaching job in Flatbush, and George received a penny a line for writing articles in his spare time.

Not until he went to work on the *Tribune* did he manage to pay off his creditors. His salary as book reviewer was five dollars a week, then eight, ten, fifteen, and twenty-five until the outbreak of the Civil War. Although Ripley didn't know it then, his "Reviews of New Books" set a pattern which, in one way or another, is now followed by approximately 304 out of 1,780 daily newspapers. It offered something new to the average reader just as Outcault did with the funnies. Under Ripley's guidance the *Tribune's* book review section became a model for daily newspapers in other parts of the country.

It is unnecessary to recall such distinguished reviewers and critics before him as Jared Sparks, Edgar Allan Poe and William Cullen Bryant. Unlike Ripley, they discussed books haphazardously in journals of limited circulation. They did not have any influence on the book trade. Nathaniel Hawthorne, for example, failed to secure through *Mosses from an Old Manse* any favor with the few critics in existence or with the reading public. The fault was evidently not with the book, which has been properly placed among his masterpieces, but with the lack of understanding or appreciation on the part of the public.

The Scarlet Letter was the first of Hawthorne's novels to appear after Ripley became one of the *Tribune's* special features. "The weird and ghostly legends of the Puritanic history present a singularly congenial field for the exercise of Mr. Hawthorne's peculiar genius," Ripley wrote in the country's most exciting daily. "He derives the same terrible excitement from these legendary horrors, as was drawn by Edgar Poe from the depths of his own dark and perilous imagination, and brings before us pictures of death-like, but

329

strangely fascinating agony, which are described with the same minuteness of finish—the same slow and fatal accumulation of details—the same exquisite coolness of coloring, while everything creeps forward with irresistable certainty to a soul-harrowing climax, which made the last-named writer such a consummate master of the horrible and infernal in fictitious composition. Hawthorne's tragedies, however, are always motivated with a wonderful insight and skill to which the intellect of Poe was a stranger."

Hawthorne, in his forty-sixth year, found himself, for the first time in American literature, the winner of a mass audience. *The Scarlet Letter* was a huge success. It gave him a chance to devote all his time to creative writing. The enthusiasm for Hawthorne might have faded had not Ripley used his position to bolster it when *House of the Seven Gables* appeared in 1851.

"It is possible that some of the most fervent admirers of Hawthorne may complain of a falling off in the construction of this romance," the *Tribune* reviewer said, "and miss the tragic pathos which is exchanged for an artistic development of the gentler affections. But this objection will scarcely be felt on a second reading ... The 'House of the Seven Gables' is certainly not inferior to any of his former productions."

Odd as it seems, no book reviewer played a more prominent part in the flowering of New England writers than Ripley. That he knew many of them personally had nothing to do with his estimate of their literary work. He judged the books under review without fear or favor, and he wrote with objectivity and deep critical acumen. In all his reviews he tried his utmost to pick out the most significant passages in a book, and the extracts enabled the readers to judge the quality of the work for themselves.

At every turn he disclosed the extent of his reading. Reviewing Henry James' *Moralism and Christianity* he invoked the names of Swedenborg, Kant, Wordsworth, Coleridge, Carlyle, and Fourier. He compared the somber scenes in *The Scarlet Letter* with the similar productions of Goethe and Scott. "If we had never heard of Mr. Melville before," he said in a review of Herman Melville's *Mardi*, "we should soon have laid aside the book as a monstrous compound of Carlyle, Jean-Paul, and Stern, with now and then a touch of Ossian thrown in." He was the most distinguished critic of New York, if not of the country, and as such had something compelling to say about every major writer of his time.

"His writings," he remarked in a review of Emerson's *Representative Men*, "possess the

331

sparkling freshness of a salient fountain   they
seem so redolent of all delicious aromas, that
they might even allure the swarm of bees that
rested on the mouth of Plato." A longer analysis,
though not necessarily more sincere, was one on
Mahomet and His Succesors, by Washington
Irving. Ripley wrote, "We scarcely need say that
in a department of literary effort, so congenial
to the studies and tastes of the admirable author,
we find the same flowing beauty of expression
and felicitious grouping of individuals and
events, which give such a magic charm to every
production of his honey-dropping pen."

Ripley won the high place assigned to him as
a book reviewer by familiarity with all sorts of
literature; by the facility with which he touched
upon myriads of subjects, from economics and
theology, philosophy and science, to the dramas,
poems and novels that came along. He back-
grounded all this with a very extensive scholarship in many fields, for he had read widely in
French, German, Greek, Italian, and English
literature. Thus he was often able to identify the
derivation of new work.

No sooner had his influence spread than
writers outside of New England who were eager
to have their work associated with Hawthorne,
Emerson, Thoreau, and Longfellow started to

send their manuscripts to New York publishers. Pretty soon New York won pre-eminence in the quantity and in the importance of its literary output. At Harper & Brothers, where Ripley was literary adviser and reader, the influx of new manuscripts was enormous. The four Methodist brothers converted Ripley's idea into magazine form and engaged him to conduct the literary department of Harper's Monthly. All these changes were very important in emphasizing New York as a literary center and in bringing the influence of Ripley and other book critics to bear upon the work of encouraging American authorship.

Yet Ripley himself was utterly without literary ambition. Rev. William Henry Channing often urged him to write a book dealing with his experiences at Brook Farm, but he always laughed uproariously at the suggestion. Ripley was 78 years old when the Unitarian minister again asked him, "When will you tell the story, as you alone can tell it?" The gray-haired bookman, with a twinkle in his black eyes, replied, "When I reach my years of indiscretion!"

During these years he collaborated with three men in book productions. The first of these was Bayard Taylor, a wiry, adventurous Quaker, endowed with real physical courage and the literary ability of a poet. Ripley's wide acquaintance with both early and modern literature, and Taylor's keen critical sense of the fine arts, prompted them to select and publish a volume known as "Handbook of Literature and Fine Arts." George Palmer Putnam published the 650-page book in 1852.

Before that Taylor entered a contest held by Phineas T. Barnum to find the words of an original song which Jenny Lind might sing at her first appearance in America. Ripley, with whom Taylor worked side by side on the *Tribune*, and Putnam, his publisher, were on the board of judges. In response several hundred poems were sent in. The judges, however, were unable to decide between Taylor's ode and that of another contestant, although Ripley and Putnam naturally favored Taylor's "Greeting to America." "Let Jenny decide," said Barnum. The Swedish songstress read both entries and selected—guess, you're right—Taylor's song.

The success which crowned the "Handbook of Literature and Fine Art" soon led to another and far more ambitious undertaking. His second collaborator was Charles A. Dana, managing editor of the New York *Tribune*. Probably no two men were better qualified to undertake the preparation of an American cyclopedia. Dana, whom

Ripley first met when he came to Brook Farm to teach Greek and German, had stored his mind as much as Ripley with an extraordinary variety and amount of learning.

A cyclopedia was a work of considerable scope. The publishers, D. Appleton & Co., did all they could do to facilitate the project. As editor in chief, Ripley selected the best known authorities to write on each subject and members of his staff to cull books of reference for material not covered by the authorities. To it he gave every hour he could spare from his literary criticism. He made notes in a memorandum-book to make sure that no piece of valuable information would be omitted. He went over each article with the same editorial care, and, as far as could be, the same critical acumen which went into his book criticism. He gave each subject only as much space as it deserved, some of which had to be increased or cut according to its importance. Ripley and Dana devoted the rest of the time to correction of statements or of style. They wanted to exclude individual peculiarities and opinions.

The first volume of the American Cyclopedia was published in 1858, and the rest followed at regular intervals until the sixteenth volume was finished in 1862. The entire set was thoroughly revised in 1873-76, and then Ripley continued to condense the revised edition into four volumes. Altogether the sales of all editions hit the million mark in the first decade.

Face to face with Ripley one would not imagine that he was a lily-livered bookworm. He fairly oozed vitality, he radiated merriment, he laughed and talked in a way that made everyone cheerful and buoyant. After arriving at work he exchanged banter with his fellow-workers and then went to work. He would sit in his chair all day long, reading and writing, unconscious of fatigue, heedless of the noise of the presses, and page after page of manuscript piled up on his desk like magic. Often he stole away from his office like a truant schoolboy to go for a swim at Coney Island.

When his wife died from cancer in 1861, Ripley for the first time in his life found himself lonely and depressed. Yet so intent was he on his scholarly pursuits that he tried to bury his solitude in work. He grappled with the final volumes of the American Cyclopedia. In 1865 he married Louise Schlossberger, a young German divorcee who supported herself and nine-year-old child by teaching music, and she quickly brought order and comfort into his life. She brought him out of seclusion, got him to mix with people, and took him on sightseeing trips. During his last years they traveled abroad and he interviewed scientific and literary notables of foreign lands.

Despite the success of the American Cyclopedia, Ripley stayed on the *Tribune* for thirty-one years, and in 1871 was earning $75 a week. It was at this point that the columns of Greeley's brainchild bear witness to an amazing variety of toil. Within this period came the best works of Voltaire, Rousseau, Goethe, Carlyle, and Bryant, and Ripley amazed many of his readers by distinguished criticism of great masterpieces.

His eye focused upon the literary scene, he advanced through life without letting anything divert him from his task. He worked hard but did not interrupt his tempo. He never rode when he could walk. The years put weight on his frame without modifying his habits.

Toward 1880 he was seen less frequently at the *Tribune* building; but, rising early every morning, he continued to devote the major part of his time to endless reading, meditation and writing. He lived almost entirely in his study, without exercise, and refused to go outdoors in cold weather. He was dreadfully afraid of catching cold. The fear increased his sedentary habit. He was finally stricken by a distressing illness. In the expiring agony of angina pectoris neither doctors nor loving devotion could give relief.

337

He grew gradually weaker, but his spirit retained its lucidity and power, and he continued to write reviews unceasingly. On July 4, 1880, alone in his study, settled in his armchair and writing a book review, he died.

What his biographer, Octavius B. Frothingham, wrote at the time of his death, seems to be quite true. "With him literature was a high calling, on a line with the ministry, which he abandoned, or the career of reformer, which he undertook at Brook Farm. One spirit animated all his performance from beginning to end. The forms of his activity changed; his hope and purpose continued unfaltering to the last. Whether preaching, administering, writing, making a Cyclopedia, or reviewing books, he had one end in view — the enlightenment and elevation of mankind."

Chapter Nineteen

Father of Parking Meters

Had you been standing on a certain busy corner in downtown Oklahoma City on the morning of July 17, 1935, you would have seen a very curious spectacle. Through the shopping district, with a never-ending squeal of brakes, jerked a two-day stream of automobiles. A surprising number of them halted abreast devices which looked like glass-and-metal lollipops along the curb.

From one machine stepped a tall, leather-faced oil driller and fumbled in his pockets for a nickel to insert into the mechanical hitching post which read: Park-O-Meter. When the green dial, visible through glass on two sides, failed to move up to the paid-up time mark, he kicked the two-inch pipe on which the meter was mounted and observed in a slow drawl: "Whoever thought of this damn thing should be shot."

He started to walk up the street, but before he

had a chance to go very far, a bystander grabbed his arm.

"Easy, there," he said, "Better turn your meter handle. It's easier than damning Magee."

The car parker halted. Nearly everyone in Oklahoma City, out where quick-tempered men followed gunplay as much as oil wells, heard about Carl C. Magee, one of the most crusading — and some say fearless — editors ever to set foot in the Southwest country. Yet few knew that he fathered the most noteworthy idea in traffic control since the birth of the traffic light. Naturally Oklahomans were surprised to find 174 of his parking meters on the north side of Main Street.

From 7 a. m. to 6 p. m. policemen had to go around and show confused motorists how to use them. Then the parkers dropped nickels into the slots and turned small handles on the side of the timing mechanisms until white pointers registered sixty minutes. As the car owners hurried off to the stores to do their shopping or pay bills in office buildings, the white arrows began to slip slowly across the dial. When the paid-for time elapsed, the green flags dropped out of sight and red ones marked VIOLATION popped up in their places.

The thirteenth year after Magee took up the

parking meters, motorists were putting more than $40,000,000 in parking meters in approximately 1500 U. S. cities and towns. The tax collector of Sacramento, California, took the largest share with $231,000 from 2,300 meters. The meters sold themselves on merit. In the 2,200 cities where they are now used, motorists find it easier to find a place to transact their business quickly. The long-time parker has removed his car to a lot or garage or out of the busy district There are less abuses of parking privileges.

It all started in 1934 when the Oklahoma City Chamber of Commerce decided to do something about the local traffic problem. It asked Carl Magee, editor of the *Oklahoma News*, a Scripps-Howard daily, to head a fact-finding committee. A familiar sight downtown was this towering, raw-boned man, crumpled felt hat on his head and copy paper sticking out of his coat pockets as he shuttled back and forth between his editorial sanctum and the city's store-laden area. At the sprightly age of sixty-one, the powerfully-built editor, with salt-and-pepper hair, a benign smile and rimless-steel glasses carried such a robust schedule that many associates found it difficult to keep up with him. With the help of others he found that people who worked in the busy downtown section arrived early in the morning and left their cars in a busy area all day long. As a result there wasn't enough parking space for persons who came downtown on business or to go shopping.

When he returned with his report, Magee brought the business leaders up rigidly in their seats by suggesting a system of timing the parking hogs. They knew him as a man who could dig up facts, but they did not think he could invent a mechanical gadget to sell parking time to motorists. The traffic control advocate, once a teacher and lawyer, talked about his idea with the calm of a six-day bicycle racer saving his wind for a long, stiff grind but confident of ultimate victory. Many businessmen were skeptical, but Magee wasn't. He finally took the matter into his own hands.

As a young man, he learned to work with tools. Once he made a self-starter for automobiles, but he never put it on the market. Now things were different; he wanted to invent a parking meter to put on the market. A rather unsung mechanic, with a lock of hair forever hanging over his studious eyes, he worked on designs of parking regulators until it interfered with his other duties. Then he offered $3,000 to postgraduate students of the Oklahoma Agriculture and Mechanical College to devise a slot-machine meter for use on public streets.

After making the offer, he realized he would not be able to sell parking meters and work for the *Oklahoma News* at the same time. He quit his editorial post and raised $50,000 among his friends to start the Dual Parking Meter Company. He took the first model out of a college lab and sent it to Tulsa, where precision machine manufacturers made as many meters as he needed.

As president of the Dual Parking Meter Company, so called because the meter aimed 1. to control parking and 2. provide revenue, Magee displayed an immense knowledge of municipal affairs, organization and problems. He sat down with A. P. Van Meter, assistant municipal counselor, and W. H. Brown, special counsel, to prepare an ordinance permitting the operation of parking meters on the streets. He realized that the ordinance would be tested later in the courts. After that he went to work on the City Council.

As his workmen were painting white lines twenty-feet apart and installing a parking meter above the pavement in each interval, the City Council still hadn't confirmed the parking meter contract. The city did not have to pay a cent of the installation costs, yet the councilmen hesitated to act in the face of public opposition. Magee agreed to take 85 per cent of the receipts until the meters, $58 each, were paid for and became the property of the city. On July 16, when the councilmen finally voted five to two in favor of the contract, the city authorities and Magee had trouble on their hands.

At first some motorists tried to buck the space dispensers. They parked in one stall after another without dropping a nickel into the parking meters in order to make a test case of the new ordinance. Four young men set up a card table in one of the parking spaces for a game of bridge. Another man tied a dog to a parking meter. Chief of Police John Watt took everything with a grain of salt. "We are not arresting anyone until the public can get accustomed to the system," he said. The third day a lawyer named Butterfield, who tried to get a ticket on Monday and Tuesday, stormed into district court to obtain an injunction against collection of parking nickels and subpenas for the appearance of Magee and two city officials in court.

Facing a judge or fighting for his rights was nothing new to Magee. He was born in Fayette, Iowa, on January 5, 1873. His father, a roving Methodist minister, taught him to use his fists in self-defense, never to accept a slight from anyone, but to tell the truth and lead a clean life. Magee owed much of his civic spirit to this training. Equally significant is the fact that after becoming a schoolteacher with degrees from Iowa State Teachers' College and Upper Iowa University, he rose to the superintendency of schools at Carroll, Iowa, and never knew the kick of taking part in public affairs.

His awakening came about unexpectedly. His wife, whom he married in 1895, became ill with tuberculosis at a time when he was flowering in law. After leaving Iowa and spending 17 years in a successful law practice in Tulsa, Oklahoma, he moved to New Mexico, principally for his wife's health, and made a deal for the *Albuquerque Morning Journal.* His probing mind soon loaded his editorial columns with dynamite. His exposure of a $100,000 deal between President Harding's Secretary of the Interior, Albert B. Fall, and wealthy oilman Harry Sinclair for leasing some naval oil reserves including Teapot Dome, led to the worst scandal that ever smirched the Presidency of the United States. Magee's devotion to the truth, however, cost him his first newspaper, involved him in two libel suits, a jail sentence, broken windows of his home, assaults upon him in the halls of the state capital, threats with loaded weapons, a killing and trial and acquittal for accidental manslaughter. By July 23, 1935, he was pretty familiar with courts.

When the parking meter case came up in district court that morning, Magee sat between two city officials as Ed Butterfield contended the parking meters sold to a few citizens the use of streets which belonged to all. And the plaintiff, stealing a look at Magee, objected to the new regulators because it enriched a private company by municipal ordinance. Then it was Magee's turn.

Looking around the courtroom, the fireless firebrand saw representatives of the street railway company which favored the meters. Beside them Magee saw merchants who liked the idea of keeping the curb clear for the carriage trade. All over the courtroom he saw persons who did not want meters removed from the streets. He felt as he did a few days earlier when he took the meter boxes from standards and said, "Everything will be all right." After hearing what he had to say about the enforcement of the ordinance, the popularity of meters with motorists who wanted to transact business quickly in town and the collection of nickels for the maintenance and upkeep of the meters, the court ordered the parking devices restored.

The victory spurred Magee to greater efforts. About two weeks later, the Oklahoma City Council voted to install parking meters on the opposite sides of streets on which they already were located and in other parts of the business district. Dallas and El Paso, Texas, lengthened the parade of curb slot machines. Then St. Petersburg, Florida. "No matter where I went," said Magee upon return from a selling trip to several major cities, "the most talked of subject was park-o-meters."

Magee returned home only to find that someone else had taken the parking meter ordinance into court again. He was not worried. The persons who objected to parking meters were not as tough as some he met as an editor. Take Judge D. J. Leahy, for example. Back in New Mexico, he convicted Magee on charges of criminal libel for his blistering editorials and sentenced him to a year in prison. The Governor pardoned him.

Despite the pardon, Judge Leahy threatened to make Magee pay for his attacks upon his handling of court cases. One day in the lobby of a Las Vegas hotel he spotted the newspaper crusader being interviewed by a local woman reporter. He approached as near as he could to give the impression of walking past them and then swung around with a haymaker up on Magee's neck. The blow dislocated the editor's vertebrae and knocked him to the floor. As he landed, Magee's .25 calibre automatic fell in front of him. The jurist pounced on him so that he could not grab his gun. He lay helpless on the floor until one of his friends, John B. Lassiter, intervened. Just as he pulled Leahy off the editor, Magee retrieved the gun and fired blindly. He shot Leahy in the arm and killed Lassiter. He was tried for the accidental slaying of Lassiter and acquitted.

The case in Oklahoma was mild in comparison. The automobilist, H. E. Duncan, who claimed that parking meters created an illegal obstruction to traffic, resorted to legal channels to take the case up to the Oklahoma Supreme Court. The judicial body upheld the ordinance that Magee helped to write. The verdict started a wave of meter installations across the country.

It was then that Magee stepped out of the picture for a while. His wife died and he left the state capital to edit a string of newspapers in the fertile Rio Grande valley. Some of Magee's friends thought he was crazy to throw away what looked like one of the biggest futures in the traffic control business. Others thought it would have been all right to quit if only he knew what he was going to do with himself. He became a crusader for a stabilized citrus industry and improvement of the water supply, but in 1941 he withdrew from southern Texas.

He returned to Oklahoma City a changed

man. The years away his old haunts whitened Magee's hair. He lost control of the Dual Parking Meter Company to some eastern industrialists. Night after night he paced the floor of his bedroom in the Oklahoma Club and wondered what to do. With the outbreak of World War II, he no longer wondered. The manufacture of parking meters was halted, and the equipment devoted to war materials. Indestructible public servant, with talent to match, he organized the State War Fund and headed the yearly bond campaigns. Then, in plain, somber clothes after warwork, he taught a Methodist Sunday school.

When the war ended, he and Gerald A. Hale leased a plant in Oklahoma City to turn out an automatic parking meter. Although it had a growing staff of parking meter salesmen, the Magee-Hale Park-O-Meter faced stiff competition from other manufacturers who entered the field. Salesmen vied with one another for city contracts because they knew that once they were in they were in for good.

No man knew the battle of cities against automobiles as well, or surveyed likely spots for parking meters as tirelessly, as the six-foot-one president of Magee-Hale. To meet the postwar demand for parking meters, he worked longer hours to increase production. Then all of a sudden he was stricken with the flu. Friends urged him to stay home and rest but he wouldn't. He was finally taken to St. Anthony's hospital, and put under an oxygen tent. He died on January 31, 1946, and was succeeded in the business by his 36-year-old son Ted.

The Magee-Hale company hung on as parking meter manufacturers began bidding recklessly for contracts. The postwar output of new cars put such a strain on long-inadequate street parking facilities that hundreds of cities and towns turned to Magee's brainchild for relief. The boom gained such momentum that from 1945 to 1949 the number of parking meters in operation in the United States jumped from 200,000 to 700,000.

The meters multiplied so fast that some traffic policemen could not keep up with them. One day in Oklahoma City, the municipality that Magee supplied with all its meters, a woman shopper found a parking meter on the curb and a ticket on the windshield of her car for not depositing a nickel. She marched down to the traffic court and almost raised the roof off the place. An investigation by the police judge showed that there was no meter there when the woman parked her car.

Since the first ones were installed in Magee's

home town, motorists have found countless ways
of parking in a metered area without paying and
cities now conduct experiments to see whether
any machine can be manipulated with a bobby-
pin, a paper clip or even a piece of cardboard and
then order the machine which appears to be fool-
proof. Not so long ago in Philadelphia, several
parking meter salesmen treated city officials to
a gadget show and a discussion of the relative
security of parking meters against motorists who
use slugs and other contrivances. Asked if the
Park-O-Meter had failed to meet certain specifi-
cations, Ted Magee said, "Yes, like any other
machine, it can be jimmied."

"What do you mean?" the presiding judge
asked.

"By jimmied," he said, "slugs or other things
could be put in to spring the timing mechanism
so you get free parking. But stealing of time has
never been an important factor in the operation
of parking meters. More dimes are put in by mistake than are slugs by people trying to beat the
meter."

Magee's important contribution to the auto-
moblie age wasn't, as he often said, the cure-all
for traffic jams. It was only to make motorists
conscious of the time they are parked and put an
end to all-day parking. Faster turnover of cars

make space more readily available for shoppers and traders in the marketing, industrial and business centers of a community. Which is just what Carl Magee predicted for his mechanical marvel.

Chapter Twenty

Father of the Permanent Wave

Hairdressing is big business.

Never before in history have so many women cared to visit the beauty shops to get permanent waves, dyeing and tinting, shampooing and scalp treatments. In 1915 there were only three hairdressers in the United States that made enough money to pay income taxes. Today there are 75,111 beauty shop owners who take in annually about $417,570,000 and pay out in wages about $143,274,000. The permanent wave appeared on the market in 1905 and has enjoyed the biggest boom of any hairdressing product in history.

Millions of women who have benefited from this remarkable invention in one form or another haven't had a chance to express their gratitude to the German hairdresser who transformed their way of life—because few know who he was and because he died in 1951 without any mention of him in *Who's Who* or the *Dictionary of American Biography*.

The father of this bloodless revolution was Charles Nessler, who was born at Schonau, a small shoe manufacturing town in southern Germany, on May 1, 1872, one in a family of five girls and three boys. Charles was a normally bright lad; he attended the village school in Todtnau, four miles away, and liked to play with girls as well as boys. With a shortage of boys at times when he wanted to play rounders, he enlisted girls to chase the ball and backstop. One day, however, his pet sister could not play because she had to put up her hair in unsightly rag curlers in preparation for a social event. The reason for her absence amused a little girl with golden curls who served as a ball chaser.

"I just hold my head in the steam from the kettle," she giggled, "and it curls right away."

Subsequently Charles followed the vagaries and mysteries of hair as surely as his brothers grew up in their father's trade of shoemaking. One day he applied steam to see what, if anything, it would do to his sister's hair. It stirred up a family scene, and his sister went back to rag curlers.

Not long afterwards he went to visit a sick aunt. He could hardly believe his eyes when he was within range of her bedside. Her hair wasn't combed and hung down like a wet mop. When she got over her bout with rheumatic fever, he went back to see her again and was even more surprised. Her hair, which before could not hold curls for more than a few hours, was curly and remained so for months.

Very early, conscious of his intellectual precocity and interest in hair, he began to live in visions of hair culture. At the age of fourteen he packed his few personal belongings in a knapsack and wandered down the Wiesental valley to Basil, Switzerland, where he became a barber's apprentice. In addition to sweeping the floor and looking after supplies, he learned to cut hair with one hand and pull teeth with the other. In those days barbers were called upon to do either service. From there he went to Geneva, settled down long enough to learn that he was a descendant of a Swiss poet, then moved to Paris.

By the time he was seventeen he knew enough about hair to find employment in a coiffeur's shop. He took to hairdressing the way Dewey took to arranging books, Shields to first aid training, Outcault to drawing comics and Ripley to book reviewing; he became trained in the mechanics of hair styles the way McParlan was trained in the mechanics of labor espionage or Jenney in architecture. At the same time he took to reading De

Maupassant, a contemporary writer who showered the human juices of French life on the reading public, and admired him the rest of his life as though they had been friends in Paris.

Nessler never met DeMaupassant. He moved to London, the center of English life, and finding that there was little hairdressing work to be had, became a wigmaker. He was deluged with hair of all types. On one occasion when he fell off a bicycle on an English roadside, he invented artificial eyelashes out of processed hair to protect his eyes from flying specks of dirt. But his biggest problem was to find the secret of curling and waving hair so that he could give permanent waves.

Hardly had the news of the discovery of artificial eyelashes reached the world when an accident of great importance happened one night in the workshop of Nessler's hair emporium. He took a strand of hair, daubed it with borax paste, wrapped it up in paper and tin foil, and curled it with heated gas irons for several minutes. Then he dipped it into hot water. The strand of hair stayed curly.

Still the inventor had months of struggle ahead of him. He tried the same formula on another strand of hair. It didn't work. The hair became straight after he took it out of the hot water. He worked all night on various other strands but without success. He thought of the lucky curl again. Why did it stay curled? He came to the conclusion that somehow the heated borax and water got into the pores of the hair shaft and maintained the wave. He figured he had the answer if he could find a process which would loosen the hair shaft cells.

From this accidental observation came a train of tests which culminated in the triumphal work of Charles Nessler. With the patience of 1,000 miles, he went to his stockpile of processed hair and selected every variety of hair texture he could find. He stayed up late every night until he created porosity in hundreds of hair samples by the forcible injection of borax. His failures grew fewer. Gradually he succeeded in waving nine out of ten varieties by the same process.

One day in 1906 he demonstrated the permanent wave process successfuly before a large crowd in London. An eminent Russian biologist by the name of Elie Metchnikoff, one of the spectators, exclaimed that it was "the greatest greatest advance ever made in hair science."

England marveled at the news. Here was another way to make women more attractive to men. Hairdressers were bewildered. A man had not only pushed back the frontiers of hair sci-

ence—but a miracle man had arisen who could
curl hair so that it would stay curled for life.
He was living in the reign of King Edward VII,
in the age of gaslights, ice wagons and bloomers.
Few beauty parlors were in existence. Marcel,
who had developed the iron curler, died penniless because women would not abandon rag
curlers.

Then began the parade of straight-haired
women to Nessler's place of business. The shop,
a few steps below the street level, was quickly
changed into a beauty parlor. From every corner of England came women to have their hair
waved as only Nessler could do it. Among them
were Queen Alexandra, who had married the
English king at the time he was Prince Albert,
and other members of the English royal family.
He fully expected that one wave treatment was
all that they would need in their lives.

But later Nessler found more than he had
expected. Some of the women who had received
permanent waves returned to the shop to heap
indignation, reproach and tears of disappoint-
ment upon the "miracle man." The curliness of
the hair close to the scalp had disappeared. He
could not understand this! Had the women
washed their hair with a strong solution? He
gave them another permanent wave and asked

them to return in two months. The same effect was noticed. He repeated the waving process with other women, and in every case the permanent wave lasted longer at the ends than at the hair roots.

He suspected that hair grew out of the roots and naturally the straight hair that he saw was not hair that he had curled. It was a new growth of straight hair. But he could not lay his hands on any scientific authority to support his theory.

Nessler did not limit himself to Great Britain. Like a wandering vendor of medicine, he took his portable equipment across the English Channel to give permanent waves to the Kaiser's wife and other members of royalty. Along with his hairdressing he became a salesman of permanent wave machines. He took delight in seeing foreign nations, one after another, adopt his invention. In 1910, when he changed from gas to electrically heated machine, he looked forward to the United States as a market. He sent an agent to sell the permanent waves machines, but orders were slow from the United States.

In his early years in London, Nessler met a woman seven years younger than himself. She was Katherine Liable, a warm, friendly person who came from Germany to become a governess in an English household. They were married before

Nessler patented his permanent wave machine. To become even more valuable to him, his wife entered the hairdressing business to handle appointments.

Other husbands might have been satisfied with making enough money to support a family. But not Nessler. He kept treating hair to see what it needed for self-curling. He probably experimented on his two daughters, Rosa and Catherine, when they were babies and in 1912 finally found a formula for self curling hair in babies. Instead of using a permanent wave machine, he dissolved a tablespoon of borax and a tablespoon of glycerin in a pint of water and applied it to an infant's scalp several times daily. After each application, he pushed the wet hair toward the roots and covered it with a net to prevent the hair from taking a straight position between one wetting and the next. Many of his clients applied the formula to their babies with success.

He had spent about 16 years in England when events suddenly altered his life. War broke out in Europe. As a German national in the English capital, the 42-year-old hairdresser found himself in a delicate position. The English government started to intern Germans on the Isle of Man, and before it reached the merchants Nes-

sler went to the British authorities and explained
that he had more than 30 employees who depended upon his business for a livelihood. With
their families the number swelled to 135. If he
were interned, they would lose their means of
livelihood. He asked permission to go to the
United States and open a branch office, thereby
keeping the British end of the business out of
German hands.

He left his wife and four children in London
and embarked for the United States. The family
followed him five years later. On arriving at New
York, he rented a booth in a hairdresser's shop
on 42nd Street, near Fifth Avenue, and put
$2,000 which he had smuggled out of England
into one advertisement in the New York *Times*.
He adopted *Nestle* in his business name because
it was better known than Nessler. From *grande
dames*, society leaders and actresses came inquir-
ies about the permanent wave. He impressed
them with his sincere talk and knowledge of hair
and kindled their imagination with his salesmanship.

These inquirors at first visited him out of
curiosity. But when they returned to their old
haunts with their hair done up in the latest style,
others followed. Before the first year was over,
Nessler had coiffured such celebrities as Mrs.

Vanderbilt and Mrs. Gould. Fortunately all his permanent waves were successful. From then on his reputation was assured.

The women of New York declared him to be the most colorful hairdresser ever to walk off a gangplank when he arrived there in 1915, yet in his soft, modulated voice they traced a slow plodding and pedestrian German accent. The shaggy-haired specialist looked like a tintype of a German professor. Weighing 160 pounds of solid flesh and standing up five feet, seven inches, in unfailing health and good spirits, he had a big symetrical head and a full face, with an aquiline nose, bristling eyebrows and washed out blue eyes, kindly, sincere and direct in their gaze. His jaw was large and curved; he wore a good-sized mustache. His skin was fresh and unwrinkled. Everything about him gave the impression of supreme confidence; his erect body, his easy, straightforward manner, his settled maturity.

It was not surprising, therefore, that within two years his business outgrew the suite on Forty-second Street and two years later one at 657 Fifth Avenue. In 1920 he bought with $50,000 in cash and a $200,000 mortgage the building at 12-14 East 49th Street, once a private dance hall, which he converted into a beauty salon with 48 booths.

FATHER OF THE PERMANENT WAVE

He regarded himself as a hairdresser. In truth, his friends liked to joke that he was more interested in permanent waving than in making money. Brusque and domineering in his own home, he would put on an unctuous, ingratiating, Emily Post manner at the approach of a lady who wanted a permanent wave. One of his operators would curl a strand of her hair to see how much heat it could absorb and then call Father Nessler, as he was affectionately known, to examine the test curl. He brushed no customer aside, but gave each one his personal attention. The wife of a ditchdigger, if she could afford $60 for a permanent wave, received the same attention as Mrs. Woodrow Wilson.

With women flocking to get Nestle permanent waves, the super-charged son of a German shoemaker opened a branch with 60 booths at 1650 Broadway in 1923. To operate the machines he held instruction classes for job applicants. Wig blocks were set up on long tables. Each student, under Nessler's instructions, learned to curl the wigs perfectly before he was graduated from the school into a well-paying job. The school was the godfather of the independent schools of beauticulture now in existence.

The more women came to the beauty parlors the more complaints were heard about permanent waves. In many cases the borax used in the waving process made the hair harsh and stiff. Nessler discussed the problem with his chief chemist, Henry Wenzel, and they worked together on other substitutes until the simon-pure inventor got the idea to try the fatty substance known as lanolin obtained from sheep. As a result the Lanoil wave was found in 1923.

Nessler advertised it heavily, building up the consumer demand, and by 1924 his advertising bill amounted to quarter of a million dollars a year. At the end of the second year he began producing Lanoil home permanents on a large scale. Sales offices were opened in Chicago, Atlanta, Boston, Cleveland, Detroit, Minneapolis, New Orleans, Philadelphia, St. Louis and San Francisco to push the home outfits at $15 a set. He opened a factory on Long Island to turn out flannels impregnated with lanolin and permanent waving machines and put it in charge of his oldest son, Charles Nessler, Jr., a conceited, publicity-shy man of mediocre business ability.

The creator of feminine beauty used still another method in the marketing of his permanent wave machines, namely, the hairdressers' exhibitions. In 1923, when the first permanent wave show was held at New York's fabulous Waldorf Hotel, the hair of twelve girls were permanently curled free of charge. Nessler was a practical showman and built up a tremendous fortune which represented only a small part of his contribution to the world. Up to 1925 he sold 100,000 machines from $300 to $750 apiece. They were found in 5,000 beauty parlors which employed about 20,000 persons.

Tales of fortunes to be reaped with the permanent wave machines fired thousands of housewives to enter the hairdressing field. Many of them converted the front rooms of their homes into beauty parlors. Lack of sufficient training on the part of these entrepreneurs weakened public goodwill and was a drawback in the commercial exploitation of permanent wave machines. As president at the time of the American Master Hairdressers Association, Nessler supported a bill in New York State which required that operators of a beauty parlor have three years of practical experience before opening up a business. More than 30 states now have a law which requires operators to pass a State examination in the technique of wielding irons and intricacies of permanent waving.

Not all the trouble was at the door of inexperienced operators. Still more vital, Nessler found that there were unsuspected varieties of human hair which responded excellently to the Lanoil treatment and others which were detrimentally affected. In other words, unless an operator could buy an alkaline solution to match the porosity of hair, she would always have trouble with easy-to-wave and hard-to-wave hair.

Nessler felt that he was born into the world with certain things to do. Some of these things were profitable and some of them were not, but he gave as much energy and attention to the one as to the other. For instance, he had two beauty salons that netted as much as $2,000 a day and a hair laboratory that cost him hundreds of dollars a week to operate. Yet he had to keep it to extend his knowedge of hair, to protect his patents, and to maintain the Nestle specialty. To contend with the texture of hair he experimented with hair from thousands of heads.

He could not have done anything else. It was as natural for him to study hair as for Babe Ruth to swing a baseball bat or for Audubon to paint birds. Once, in 1926, when he was sitting behind his littered desk, reflecting, he said to a friend, "some hair absorbs 100 per cent of its own weight, some 80 per cent, some 10 per cent or less." He made the announcement as though he had a system of hair classification, but he did not cling very long to this discovery. It required too much skill and training to use in a beauty parlor. Instead, he invented a textometer to measure the elastic strength of hair under weight and separated the texture of hair into ten classifications. Because each classification required a different strength of alkaline solution, he remedied the defect of the single-strength Lanoil preparation by graduating the chemical contents and calling it Circulin. After that it was possible, if the texture of hair were known, to wave it without damage. Nessler did not sell enough of the instruments to pay for the experimental work, but it advanced permanent waving more than anyone ever before realized.

Not until 1924, when he was firmly established, did Nessler give attention to personal enjoyment. He grew tired of living in a New York penthouse and bought the old Blauvelt farm at Nanuet, New York, on which he raised animals. Three years later, in 1927, he moved to a 25-room house at Palisades, seven miles away, and in time enlarged the farm to 64 acres. Altogether it cost him $103,000. He was interested in painting and golfing. At one time he owned a herd of 30 or 35 deer. He had a bowling alley for his guests and a tennis court. His farm became a show place.

For his wife and children no expenditure seemed too great. He had a penthouse in New York City, a $60,000 mansion at Palm Beach, Florida,

and the glitting mansion at Palisades. His oldest
daughter, Rosa, a well-educated, strong-willed
artist, boasted a Cadillac coupe, as did her older
brother, Charles. The two younger children,
Catherine and John, were not as fortunate, though
they had a swimming pool and a yacht to share
with the others. The man who provided all these
luxuries, however, did not have a happy home life.
His family lived in the New York penthouse and
usually joined him at Palisades on weekends.

He spent his days in the beauty salon, super-
vising all details of permanent waving, and he
devoted his nights to finding things to do at Palisades. Daily he used to cross from New York on the
125th Street Ferry and drive home in his Cadillac
sedan. He devoted much of his leisure to writing
about hair. Within eight years he wrote three
books: *Textbook for Permanent Waving*. 1926;
The Story of Hair, 1928, and *Our Vanishing Hair*,
1934.

When Nessler needed some lines or ideas from
his associates, he would shake them gently and
start an argument. After half an hour or so, he
would call the argument off and work up the conversation into his research. He never borrowed an
idea without improving it. The one man with whom
he spent hours in discussion was Dr. Bruno Oetteking, then professor of anthropology at Columbia

University. The professor was considered aloof. To shake him out of his insularity, Nessler would take him to a restaurant down the street from his beauty salon, order a lunch, and a bottle or two of wine. The two became familiar figures among the early-afternoon crowd at the nearby restaurant.

In his fifties, the master hairdresser went out a great deal, and his chief pleasure was food and wine. One night he was halfway through a juicy steak when he jumped to his feet and offered any women in the party $1,000 if she could describe in 1,000 words her purpose in life. Any stranger would have sized him up as a bluffing millionaire. But he meant it. He would even stop an important conference to fawn upon a patron of his salon.

He was good to his employees, but woe betide the person who didn't do things as Nessler instructed him. He liked hard work and he expected hard work from them. He gave operators who made good a bonus as high as $1500 at Christmas. On one occasion shortly after he moved to Nanuet, he hired a caterer to serve his entire staff on the 35-acre estate. He had 270 employees on his payroll.

Under a bold and speculative exterior he concealed a generous nature. Once, when a borrower asked for 200 dollars, he gave it to him. Then he walked three or four miles to save a nickel subway fare. One year, shortly before he left for Berlin, he asked people to send him clothing and shoes for the suffering German people. It cost him about $3,000 to take twenty packing cases loaded with supplies to Germany.

Many hairdressers owed their success to his generosity. One of these was a man for whom Nessler paid his passage from Germany. When the man and his family reached New York, he went to work for Nessler and later opened his own beauty parlor. He was, incidently, the only hairdresser in attendance at Nessler's funeral.

The success of his inventions naturally led to many imitations. In 1928, four years after putting the Lanoil home permanent on the market, he claimed that the Le Mur Company of Cleveland, Ohio, infringed on one of his patents. Before the suit was settled, however, he sold out to the Cleveland firm for roughly two million dollars and 70,000 shares.

For several months he worked together with the new officers, but Nessler was a lone wolf who found it hard to work with a board of directors. Then too, the company had many interests, including color tints and rinses, perfumes and cosmetics, whereas Nessler thought, breathed, and lived only for hair science. No open quarrel occurred, but one day in 1929 Nessler said to the president, "Do you want to buy my stock?" Pleased at strengthening his hands, the president organized a syndicate in Cleveland to buy Nessler's stocks at $28 a share and thereafter Nessler had no partners. He received about $392,000 in cash and little more than one and a half million dollars in notes.

When Wall Street crashed a few months later, the buyers of his 70,000 shares defaulted in paying the notes. The situation was touch and go. Some of the stockholders threatened to sue Nessler for selling them the stock under false pretenses. He finally compromised. The stocks which were worth $1,572,000 some months earlier brought him about $300,000.

When the economy finally sank, the real estate Nessler purchased with the proceeds from the sale of his patent rights sank with it. He lost properties on which he held second mortgages and sacrificed others for a fraction of the original price. The undeveloped land he bought during the subdivision mania in New Jersey was eventually sold for unpaid taxes except the tracts he transferred to Pro-Ker Laboratories, Inc.

The permanent wave inventor believed in the old idea that a man can never stop learning. He insisted on discovering new inventions, looked on the bright side of things, and held to his purpose with unconquerable tenacity. Defeat only spurred him to fresh efforts. In 1932, after receiving news of government liens on one of his properties for unpaid income taxes of $168,373 for 1923, 1924, 1925 and 1926, he said, "Well, that's over, what next?"

In every problem he tackled there was contained the germ of his next invention; in every invention, the seed of his next fortune. After leaving the Nestle-Lemur Company he turned his attention to thinning hair. He designed an instrument called Kerascope to measure hair growth. The prospect of his own baldness stimulated him to find a remedy. Every Sunday morning, as he religiously counted the loss of his hair with the Kerascope, he discovered an organic waste called keratin was created from the various body parts rubbing against each other. He did not think that dandruff had anything to do with his hair loss. He asked Dr. Oetteking, who was to present the Kerascope before the American Association for the Advancement of Science in 1932, what he thought of keratin.

"Never heard of such a thing," replied the blue-eyed, textbook anthropologist.

"Can you then, perhaps, explain or at least suggest where all this keratin should come from?"

The professor who taught science of man at Columbia University for eighteen years threw up his hands. "No, I cannot," he squirmed, "and I don't see the sense in occupying yourself with that subject."

For a while Nessler thought that he had come to the end of his rope. He found he had a bad liver, and went to Europe for his health. One day, as he was resting at Carlsbad, Czechoslovakia, he heard a story about a dying dog that suddenly recovered after drinking rain water which had stagnated on a bed of coal ashes at a nearby factory. He made arrangements to send a large amount of the coal ashes to the United States for experimentation on 625 hair losers whom he had enlisted through several large advertisements in the book section of the New York *Times*. The ashes were mixed with water and other chemicals and used on the scalps of the guinea pigs. The formula had favorable results on the majority of cases who took a kerascopic examination after seven months of treatment. Nessler, who had used it too, christened the inorganic product Pro-Ker treatment.

Many of the details of Nessler's researches are obscure, and some of his valuable papers were destroyed when fire leveled his palatial mansion at Palisades in the early 1930's. It is said that his oldest daughter burned other papers after his death. But what are specific facts before the boldness and imagination of his achievements. See this inquisitive hair expert traveling from one

country to another, from the Black Forest to the
world's greatest cities by train, walking or riding
into obscure valleys, stopping at hospitals, orphan-
ages, prisons, schools and factories, examining
the heads of individuals in all walks of life with
the homely wisdom of Solomon, confounding
anthropologists, biologists and medical doctors
with his findings. Not since Galen, an eminent
Greek physician of the second century, had anyone
studied the hair-growing organism in more detail.

Nessler unfortunately lacked the wherewithal
to make the last of his sixteen inventions as popular in the household as automobiles or refrigera-
tors. In 1932 he had formed Pro-Ker Laboratories,
Inc., to handle the filtrate made from ashes and
conveyed its assets to his wife in trust for the benefit of their children. She died on June 2, 1935,
without leaving a will. At the time of her death
Mrs. Nessler held for her husband $10,963 in two
bank accounts. Charles Nessler, Jr., became the
administrator of her estate and, to the chagrin of
his father, held the money more than 14 months
without any sign of settling the estate. The elder
Nessler took the case to court.

During the hearing in Surrogate's Court at
New City, New York, held with the least amount
of publicity, it appeared that Mrs. Nessler had
contributed $232,500 to Pro-Ker Laboratories, Inc.,

largely run by her oldest son in later years, and at the time of her death the firm carried $63,998.53 on its books as accounts payable to her. The rest of her estate was valued at almost $21,000. Out of the settlement of her estate in September, 1937, the elder Nessler received about $14,000. It was hardly enough for him to do anything with the "epochal discovery" of his life on the scale to which he was accustomed.

Before the trouble with his pampered son, he had learned from his scalp experimentations that the outer skin of his body also thrived on keratin and, like hair, was always growing and shedding. He traced wrinkles, aging skin and premature baldness to the same cause. He liked to say, "Having accomplished what I wanted to accomplish and, besides, having yet another problem to take care of, the rejuvenation of skin, I lost interest in my own hair."

He made a crude device by hand and used it to apply heatless friction to his left hand. He left his other hand untreated for future comparison. The device, monogrammed with the first syllables of his name, was called Cha-Ness. From 1935 to the year of his death he used the vibrator on exposed parts of his left hand and was elated to find in time that the quality of the skin had improved. Blemishes and many liver spots had disappeared.

379

As a result he went to various manufacturers and ordered parts from his own design for 150 heatless friction machines. The first of them were sold to beauty parlors and individuals for anywhere from $150 to $370. Among the people who bought the skin rejuvenators were Ganna Walska, Metropolitan opera star, and Elizabeth Graham, a woman of beauty who graced New York society.

Nessler prided himself on his good health after the use of the Cha-Ness outfit. Only a few years before his death, however, he failed to appear one night at his boarding house in Harrington Park, New Jersey. Mrs. Russell Pratt, one of his proteges with whom he boarded off and on for about ten years, decided to drive around town and see if she could find him. No luck. Next day she learned that he had spent the night in the Closter jail. The police said he was drunk. Although Charles Nessler was not given to explanations, he felt that one was necessary in this case. "No," he muttered, "I wasn't drunk. I couldn't see the road ahead of my car, and I thought I'd just ask the first police officer I saw to drive me home. How did I know he wouldn't do it."

His eyesight, poor as it was in his youth, failed him miserably in his old age. He went to an occulist in Englewood for treatment. When he learned that the Cha-Ness machine was used on the eyes, the occulist refused to consult further with Nessler.

Even with thick horn-rimmed glasses, Nessler had trouble reading his writing. Russell Pratt, a young, intelligent man who first met Nessler shortly before his marriage to Nan Richards,managed to find a typewriter with large characters for him. Nessler spent half his time with it. Frequently he woke up with an idea in the middle of the night and devoted the rest of it working at the typewriter. He also used a large magnifying glass to read what he had pecked out on the keys.

In January, 1951, in his 79th year, he suffered his third heart attack in five years. When he recovered consciousness, he was in bed at Holy Name Hospital, in Teaneck, several miles away. He wouldn't eat or take medicine before he had a cigarette. He was as stubborn as the doctor who didn't want him to smoke. Eventually the doctor relaxed. Nessler was allowed one cigarette. He kept the cigarette dangling from his lips for 24 hours without lighting it. The twenty-first of January was the last day he had on earth. The creator of feminine beauty, who once measured his wealth in seven figures, left an estate of unsold Cha-Ness machines.

A man's last words are rarely forgotten. "If somebody asked me by what particular accomplish-

FORGOTTEN FATHERS

ment above any other I would like posterity to
remember me by, I certainly would answer: The
discovery of mechanical heatless—friction—suc-
tion and the invention of Cha-Ness." he wrote in
1948, the year before he received an award from
the American Woman's Voluntary Services for
advancing women's "economic, cultural and social
prestige." "It is my prediction that in the course
of time this device will become far more popular
than did the Permanent Wave."

ACKNOWLEDGMENTS AND SOURCES

A complete bibliography of all the books, magazines, newspapers, pamphlets and documents I have consulted in the preparation of this book would not help the reader who wants to go much deeper into the material. In many of them I found practically the same information and here I wish to include only the most important sources.

First, I am indebted to those librarians who always help a writer to bone up on his subject before he ventures out to interview people. I received friendly assistance from the staffs of the public libraries in Elizabeth, N. J., New York, N. Y., the Library of Congress, Temple University Library, the Schuylkill County Historical Society at Pottsville, the Historical Society of Pennsylvania, the Philadelphia Museum of Art, the Genealogical Society of Pennsylvania, the Colorado Historical Society, the Law Library at Philadelphia City Hall, and the public libraries in Philadelphia, Scranton, and Pottsville, particlarly Edith Patterson, who offered many useful suggestions.

It is a pleasure to express my gratitude to these persons and institutions for their friendly assistance. John J. Forbes, director of the Bureau of Mines, Dept. of Interior, Wash-

ington, D. C.; George Korson, editor of The
Red Cross Courier, Washington, D. C.; Thomas
Murphy, associate editor, Scranton Times; E. S.
Listen, secy.-treas., National Association of Inter-
collegiate Basketball, Baldwin, Kansas; John J.
Rutledge, Chief Mine Engineer, Maryland Bur-
eau of Mines; the National Archives and the
Smithsonian Institute at Washington, D. C.;
George McManus, specialist in Pennsylvania
books.

My warm thanks and appreciation for answering freely all questions put to them are due
to many men and women who were acquainted
with the fathers described in this book. Wherever
possible, wherever their information fitted into
the manuscript, I have mentioned their names
right in the text. Others are Dr. William T. Da-
vis, Nettie Hafner, Charles S. Ball, Elizabeth J.
Mundie, Mrs. David Robb, Stella Vizzard, Henry
Shields, Roy L. McCardell, James O'Dowd, Edward Stuart, Rufus Strohm, Ralph E. Weeks,
Mrs. Nellie Sammons, General Robert U. Patterson, Miss Gladys Henle, Mr. and Mrs. Russell
Pratt, Albert Schmidt, Herman Stein, Mrs. Helen
Grumpelt, Dr. Bruno Oetteking, and Mrs. Peter
Williamson.

To Edward H. Schmidt, associate editor, The
Reader's Digest on whom the criticism of this

manuscript rested particularly heavy, must go a special degree of thanks. For their helpful suggestions on one or more chapters of the book I am also indebted to Paul Trescott, editorial staff of the Philadelphia Evening Bulletin; Dr. George H. Shoaf, Costa Mesa, California; and Tom Foster, Baltimore, Md. I am grateful to R. Norris Williams, 3d, for publishing Father of the Coal Breaker in the July, 1949, issue of the *Pennsylvania Magazine of History and Biography.*

The material listed below proved especially useful.

Architecture and the Spirit of Man, by Joseph Hudnut. Cambridge, Mass., 1949.
Principles and Practice of Architecture, by W. L. B. Jenney and Sanford E. Loring. Cleveland, 1869.
The Autobiography of an Idea, by Louis H. Sullivan. New York, 1922.
Skyscraper, by Elisha H. Naumburg, New York, 1933.
Skyscrapers and the Men Who Build Them, by W. A. Starrett. New York, 1928.
Architecture in Old Chicago, by Thomas E. Tallmadge. Chicago, 1941.
Basketball: Its Origin and Development, by James D. Naismith. New York, 1941.
The Modern High School: Its Administration and Extension, Chapter High School Athletics and Gymnastics as an Expression of the Corporate Life of the High School, by James D. Naismith. New York, 1914.

Better Basketball, by Forrest C. Allen. New York, 1937
The Labor Movement: The Problem of Today, edited by
   George E. McNeill. New York, 1888.
Seventy Years of Life and Labor, by Samuel Gompers.
   2 vols. New York, 1925.
History of Philadelphia, by J. Thomas Sharf and Thompson Westcott. Philadelphia, 1884.
The Humphreys Family in America, by Fred Humphreys. New York, 1883.
Andrew Atkinson Humphreys, by Henry H. Humphreys.
   Philadelphia, 1924.
American Glass, by George S. and Helen McKearin.
   New York, 1941.
American Journalism, by Frank Luther Mott. New York,
   1942.
Comics and their Creators, by Martin Sheridan. Boston,
   1942.
Animated Pictures, by C. Francis Jenkins. Washington,
   D. C., 1898.
Boyhood of an Inventor, —Washington, D. C., 1931.
S. Parkes Cadman, Pioneer Radio Minister, by Fred
   Hamlin. New York, 1930.
Big Frogs, by Henry F. Pringle. New York, 1928.
Twenty-six years of the Life of an Actor and Manager,
   by Francis Courtney Wemyss. New York, 1847.
Dramatic Life as I Found it, by Noah M. Ludlow. St.
   Louis, 1880.
The Autobiography of Joseph Jefferson. New York,
   1890.
Two Evil Isms—Pinkertonism and Anarchism, by
   Charles A. Siringo. Chicago, 1915.
A Cowboy Detective, by Charles A. Siringo. Chicago,
   1912.
The Pinkerton Labor Spy, by Morris Friedman. New
   York, 1907.

ACKNOWLEDGMENTS AND SOURCES

The Molly Maguires and the Detectives, by Allan Pinkerton. New York, 1878.

History of the Descendants of Elder John Strong, of Northampton, Mass., by Benjamin W. Dwight. Albany, N. Y., 1871.

The Confessions and Autobiography of Harry Orchard, by Albert E. Horsley. New York, 1907.

Men and Times of the Revolution, or, Memoirs of Elkanah Watson, including Journals of Travels in Europe and America, Elkanah Watson, edited by his son, Winslow C. Watson. Dana & Co., New York, 1856.

A Tour in Holland, By an American. Printed by I. Thomas, Worcester, Mass, 1790.

A Biographical Sketch of Elkanah Watson, with a brief genealogy of the Watson family, William Reed Deane. J. Munsell, Albany, 1864.

Native Stock. The rise of the American Spirit seen in Six Lives., Arthur Pound. Macmillan, New York 1931.

The Agricultural Fair, Wayne Caldwell Neely. Columbia University Press, 1935.

George Ripley, Octavius B. Frothingham. Houghton, Mifflin & Co., Boston, 1882.

Bayard Taylor, Richard Croom Beatty. Norman, Okla., 1936.

The Life of Charles A. Dana, James H. Wilson. Harpers, New York, 1907.

Genealogy of a Part of the Ripley Family, H. W. Ripley. Newark, N. J., 1867.

R. R. Bowker, Militant Liberal, E. McClung Fleming. University of Oklahoma Press, Norman, Okla., 1952.

Melvil Dewey, Grosvenor Dawe. Lake Placid, N. Y., 1932.

Melvil Dewey, Fremont Rider. American Library Association, Chicago, 1944.

387

Textbook for Permanent Waving, by Charles Nessler. New York, 1926.

The Story of Hair, by Charles Nessler. New York, 1928.

Our Vanishing Hair, by Charles Nessler. New York, 1934.

MAGAZINES

The Father of all Skyscrapers,—Home Insurance Building. Scientific American, May, 1932.

The Origin of the Skyscraper. Architectural Record, August, 1934.

Early American Glass, by Rhea Mansfield Knittle. New York, 1927.

Christmas Clubs, by Lloyd M. Cosgrove. Quarterly Journal of Economics, August, 1927.

Christmas Savings Clubs. Literary Digest, Nov. 21, 1936.

The Man Who Invented Basketball, by M. Whitcomb Hess. The American Scholar, Winter 1948-49.

Basketball—A Game the World Plays, by James Naismith. Rotarian, January, 1939.

Three Economic Needs of the 1880's and of the 1940's, by Bishop Francis J. Haas. The American Ecclesiastical Review, Dec., 1947.

Bamboo Hut the Model of the First Skyscraper. Popular Mechanics, March, 1932.

Chicago Razes first Skyscraper. Business Week, Dec.23, 1931.

Obituary of William L. Jenney, Architectural Record, August, 1907.

The Chicago Construction, by W. L. B. Jenney. Inland Architect and News Record, Nov., 1891.

A Revolutionist Dies, Charles Nessler. Life, Feb. 5, 1951.

The Rise of T. J. Foster. Official Messenger, Oct. 10 1899.

ACKNOWLEDGMENTS AND SOURCES

Crusader for Truth, by Paul Gallico. American Weekly, July 14, 1946.

Stay Young, by Charles Nessler. Harrington Park, N. J., 1948.

Labor Day, by P. J. McGuire, American Federationist, Sept., 1902.

A Dyott Note, by Charles B. Gardner, Antiques, Oct., 1936.

Opper, Outcault and Co.,; the Comic Supplement and the Men who Make it, by R. L. McCardell. Everybody's Magazine, June, 1905.

Father of the Movies, by James B. Morrow. Ambition, 1920.

Radio Finds Its Eye, by C. Francis Jenkins, as told to Georgette Carneal. Saturday Evening Post, July 27, 1929.

A Great Preacher with a Wonderful Memory, by Thane Wilson. American Magazine, August, 1920.

Stephen C. Foster and Negro Minstrelsy, by Robert T. Nevin. Atlantic Monthly, November, 1867.

Jump Jim Crow—The Opening of an Era, by Frederick R. Sanborn. New York Times Magazine, Nov. 13, 1932.

The Father of Red Cross First Aid. The Red Cross Courier, March, 1939.

NEWSPAPERS

Stagg, at 87, Is Still Showing 'em How, by Don Donaghey. Philadelphia Sunday Bulletin, Oct. 2, 1949.

Dr. Thomas W. Dyott—Welfare Worker in the Glass Industry, by Charles Messer Stow. Boston Evening Transcript, July 23, 1927.

Story of Outcault, by R. L. McCardell. New York Telegram, January 25, 1920.

FORGOTTEN FATHERS

PAMPHLETS AND PAPERS

Correspondence of Joshua Humphreys, Collections of the Pennsylvania Historical Society.

Preface written by Dean J. Rice to *Long-Age Day* and *This Rose Will Remind You,* both songs published by J. Fischer and Bro., New York, 1931.

Gaslight from Bituminous Coal. Philadelphia., 1850.

Loeser Papers, Schuylkill County Historical Society, Pottsville, Pa.

Fifteen .Anniversary, International Correspondence Schools, Scranton, 1907.

Senate Document No. 89, 78th Congress, 1st Session, the articles written by John M. Hightower for the Associated Press on radar, 1943.

The Life of a Forgotten Giant, by A. Charles Carotis and Charles W. Phillips, Camden, 1946.

Personal Recollections of Vicksburg, by Wm. L. Jenney, Military Essays and Recollections, Military Order of the Loyal Legion of the United States, Vol. III, Chicago, 1899.

House Reports, 53d Congress, 2nd Session, Vol. 3, Report No. 902. Testimony taken by the committee of the Senate upon the Relations between Labor and Capital, 1885.

An Exposition of the System of Moral and Mental Labor, established at the Glass Factory of Dyottville, etc., by T. W. Dyott. Philadelphia, 1833.

Trial of Dr. T. W. Dyott. Philadelphia, 1839.

Date Due